REASONINGS
WITH
THE YOUTH

BLACK HISTORY, CULTURE AND POLITICS

DAVID COMISSIONG

ccip

February, 2014.

Caribbean Chapters Publishing
P.O. Box 8050, Oistins, Christ Church, Barbados
www.caribbeanchapters.com

ISBN (paperback): 978-976-95522-8-9

This book is dedicated to
my own precious 'youths':
Jutta, Aisha and Najuma;

to the wonderful young people
with whom they grew up:
the Alicias, the Ashleys, the Camilles,
Khadijah, Ziggy, Hasani,
Khalid, Bernadette, Patreece, Lauren;

to my niece and nephew, Samarah and Sharu;

to all the talented youth of the
Richard Stoute Teen Talent organization;

and to little Aiden.

Table of Contents

Introduction 1

The Roots of Emancipation in Barbados 5

Cultural Schizophrenia. 9

We Are Not Little England. 13

The Hurtful Truth About the Garrison 18

Will the Real Revolutionaries Stand Up Please? 26

A Barbadian Profile in Courage 31

The Man Who Should Have Been
    King of Barbados 35

The Inconvenient Truth About Wilberforce 41

The Slaves Who Abolished Slavery 50

Reparations I 56

Reparations II. 59

African Civilization. 62

Long Live the Pan-African Movement. 69

The Barbadian Tradition of Pan-Africanism. 75

Marcus Garvey (I). 85

Marcus Garvey (II) 89

The World's Greatest Garveyite 92

Lamming, Sobers, & Rihanna! 96

The Quiet Warrior................................... 101

We are a Caribbean Civilization 112

Barbados is the Father of Caribbean Integration 116

Historic Mistake That Must Be Corrected............. 121

The Emperor is Naked 126

Forward - in the Names of Trayvon and I'Akobi........ 130

Reasoning with the Youth 134

A Battle for the Soul of Barbados 140

A New Model of Governance for Barbados............ 146

An Emancipation Day Vision 153

Time to Do Our Best Work 158

About the Author 171

Index... 173

INTRODUCTION

BETWEEN August 1st 1834, the date on which the 1833 *British Abolition of Slavery Act* came into effect, and 1st August 1838, the date on which Barbados and several other colonies formally terminated their system of unfree labour, approximately 800,000 enslaved Africans in the British West Indies were 'emancipated'.

The dictionary definition of 'emancipation' is "liberation from bondage, disability or dependence, or from any injurious or undue restraint or influence." And yet, well over 100 years after the passage of the *Emancipation Act*, the celebrated Caribbean poet, Martin Carter was forced to ask in the title of one of his most insightful poems, *Where Are Free Men*?

Carter begins his poem with a cry of anguish:

"O we have endured such absurd times
And waited so long, so weary with time."

He also goes on to poignantly lament that:

"Since we were born our wings have had no rest
Our prison of air is worse than one of iron..."

When we examine the record of the past 170 years we are forced to admit that much of that time has been filled with absurdity—the absurdity of continuing to hold on to the coat tails of our former slave and colonial masters;

the absurdity of refusing to recognize our Caribbean encased African-ness; the absurdity of failing to look reality firmly in the face and to come together in unity to take control of our destiny; the absurdity of our continued mental enslavement. Where, indeed, are free men and women?

But it is clear that our pre-eminent Caribbean poet is intent on urging us on to more purposeful emancipatory endeavours, for he declares:

> "And what in dreams we do in life we attempt.
> But where are free men, where the endless
> streets?"

The "endless streets" are the future of self-liberation, the limitless vistas of expression and achievement that we owe to our youth and to the generations to come.

Surely, in this first decade of the 21st century it is time for us to put self-defeating folly and absurdity behind us and to fully come into the kingdom of emancipation that our revolutionary freedom fighters struggled so valiantly to attain during our wars against slavery. Surely it is time for us to liberate our minds and our collective consciousness, to dream big and magnificent dreams of self-determination, unity and achievement and to attempt to realize them in real life

It is this sacred duty and vision that has inspired this publication.

This is my heartfelt and modest gift to the youth of Barbados, the Caribbean, the Americas, the diaspora and the mother continent of Africa. I offer it as a contribution to the ongoing and historic effort to free ourselves from mental slavery.

Chapter 1

THE ROOTS OF EMANCIPATION IN BARBADOS

SUNDAY, April 14, 1816 saw the occurrence of one of the most important events in the history of Barbados, an event that ultimately led, 150 years later, to the historic happenings of November 30, 1966, the political independence of Barbados.

On that fateful Sunday, thousands of enslaved and exploited black Barbadians rose up in open rebellion against the bloody-minded, repressive, slave-holding elite that dominated Barbadian society. This rebellion, popularly known as **Bussa's Rebellion**, began in the parish of St. Philip and quickly engulfed more than half of the island.

It was eventually squashed by a combined military force consisting of the Barbadian militia and English imperial troops garrisoned in Barbados. And at the end of it all the casualties consisted of approximately 1,000 slaves killed in battle or executed in bloody reprisals.

In spite of the crushing military defeat suffered by the slaves, the rebellion was extremely significant in that it sent a clear and unmistakable message to both the local white elite and the imperial government, that the enslaved black masses of Barbados were determined to put an end to slavery in Barbados.

As noted in Dr. Hilary Beckles' Black Rebellion in Barbados, the local Whites were in no doubt about the intentions of the slaves:

> "In the words of Colonel Best, the Blacks sought 'to become masters, instead of the slaves of the island'... in support of this, Thomas Moody, a local planter, noted in October, 1816, that, the rebellion was an attempt by the mass of the slaves to gain independence."

It is significant that the planter, Thomas Moody, used the word "independence" in describing the objective that the slaves were trying to achieve. Essentially, the slaves were seeking to destroy the slave society then in existence and replace it with a new and liberating social order.

The specific features of slave society that our enslaved ancestors would have found detrimental and repressive were the denial of personal freedom to the mass of black people; their exclusion from participation in the economic system and their poverty; the comprehensive campaign to strip them of their African culture and to foist upon them a Euro-centric culture which taught them to despise themselves; and the extremely harsh and bloody system of criminal law to which they were subjected. The attempt to eradicate these negative features of Barbadian society was significantly described in 1816 as an attempt to secure "Independence".

To my mind, this constitutes an extremely important lesson that we should take to heart whenever we contemplate our formal Independence from Britain. Independence is not simply about acquiring a flag and an anthem and being able to represent ourselves at the United Nations; rather, it is about creating a new society.

The great West Indian historian, Gordon Lewis, put it this way:

> "The central reality of independence is the need to convert the patterns set by those earlier social systems (slavery and colonialism) into an independent national society run primarily in the interests of its independent citizens."

And the whole sweep of Barbadian history can legitimately be interpreted as a long and tortuous struggle on the part of the massive black labouring class to create a national society run primarily in the interest of its citizens.

From the very first landing of enslaved Africans in Barbados in 1627, one can discern a mass struggle against an exploitative and demeaning society. This struggle took many forms, ranging from acts of violent rebellion such as the **Bussa Rebellion**, to the heroic effort of enslaved blacks to engage themselves in independent economic activity in order to purchase their own freedom or alleviate their poverty.

In addition to the Bussa Rebellion, other important landmarks in the struggle were the abortive slave revolts of the 17th Century, the **Confederation Riots** of 1876, the mass emigration to Panama in the early 20th Century, the riots of 1937 and, of course, the actual attainment of Independence in 1966.

There were also outstanding individuals who played roles of varying importance in assisting the mass struggle. A short list of these would include Bussa, Samuel Jackman Prescod, Clennell Wickham, Charles Duncan O'Neal, Clement Payne, Sir Grantley Adams and the 'Father of Independence' Errol Walton Barrow.

Now that we are no longer subject to the restriction of slavery or of formal political control by the English Colonial Office, and now that formal political power rests in the hands of the representatives of the masses of Barbados, it will be to our everlasting shame if we do not fully seize the opportunity and create for ourselves the self-defined, independent society that so many of our ancestors struggled and died for.

We, the independent citizens of Barbados, must have the courage to identify all those negative aspects of our society that have held us back in the past and continue to do so; to remove them, and to erect in their place a truly Independent Barbados.

Chapter 2

CULTURAL SCHIZOPHRENIA

A FEW years ago the great Caribbean writer, George Lamming, sparked off a national debate on the issue of black consciousness and Barbadian culture.

I firmly believe that the finding of the correct 'answer' to this issue will be of crucial importance to the future progress of this young nation, and I am therefore grateful to Mr. Lamming for having raised this subject.

The starting point of any examination of the culture and consciousness of the Barbadian must be our historical experience of slavery and colonialism.

Surprisingly, while it is universally accepted that our colonial experience served to create an unnatural and distorted economic system—one in which we produce what we don't consume, and consume what we don't produce—many people find it difficult to concede that a similar distortion was created so far as our culture and our consciousness as a people are concerned.

The University of New York sociologist, Paget Henry, produced an interesting examination of this subject in his essay entitled *Decolonisation and Cultural Underdevelopment in the Commonwealth Caribbean*.

Mr. Paget makes the point that when the Europeans

first brought Africans to the Caribbean in the 17th century, they were faced with the problem of how to convert these formerly free, self-aware people into submissive slave labourers fitted for work in a plantation system. In order to bring about such a conversion, the European perceived that he would have to deal with the strong African culture which the slaves had brought with them to the Caribbean. Put simply, all African cultural traits and institutions which militated against conversion into a unit of slave labour in a plantation system would have to be removed and replaced by suitable European directed cultural traits and institutions.

Thus, the African was forbidden to practise his familiar African mode of economic productivity, and was instead taught the skills and discipline necessary to work in the oppressive slave economy.

A similar process was applied to the language of the African, to the religion of the African, and indeed to all aspects of African culture that ran counter to the African's new role as a slave labourer.

However, positive aspects of African culture did survive. They survived because they were practised in secret or survived partially, in the form of the gradually evolving hybrid creole culture of the black masses.

In addition to the attempt to deculturalise the African, other destructive processes were set in train in the colonial society. The European sought to elaborate and institutionalize in the colonial society a negative image of the black African as an unintelligent and inferior being, produced by a primitive and backward culture.

To this was then added the European rationalization of his exploitation of the African—that he was bringing civilization to the African.

The colonized black, faced with this negative image of himself, could either accept the image or he could resist it. And he could resist either negatively or positively. He could resist positively by rejecting the imposed European culture and self-image and instead seek to defend and valorize the African and Creole culture.

On the other hand, he could resist negatively by rejecting all that smacked of blackness or Africa, seeking instead to immerse himself in the culture of the European and thereby take on a European identity. This tendency towards assimilation with the European was fueled after the abolition of slavery by the new emphasis put on exposing the blacks to the Christian religion and to the colonial education system.

However, since the working-class uprisings of the 1930s, there has been a definite move to resist positively the cultural colonization to which blacks in the Caribbean have been subjected. There has been a definite attempt to shake off the warped values of the colonizer and to 'reclaim and revalorise' the hybrid creole culture, and the remnants of our original African culture.

But this attempt at cultural decolonisation has not been as successful as we would have hoped, and indeed, today, we are faced with the prospect of a reversal of the gains made, as our societies become more and more penetrated by the export culture of the United States of America.

The continuing American cultural penetration is directly linked to the fact that in our societies the vital processes of economic production are foreign dominated and oriented, and therefore lack systematic ties with our indigenous cultural system. So long as this remains the case, we will continue to suffer the onslaught of excessive foreign cultural penetration.

As a people, we are therefore faced with a monumental task of defending and promoting our own culture and our own identity.

This we must do by putting to rest, once and for all, the myth of African inferiority. And this can only be accomplished by rigorous historical scholarship and widespread public education.

In addition we must seek to infuse our society with the ethic of self-reliance and self-propelled development. A determination not to remain an economically and therefore culturally dependent people must be manifested at every level of our society, if we are to escape the ravages of cultural schizophrenia.

Chapter 3

WE ARE NOT LITTLE ENGLAND

THE mission to discover, appropriate and preserve our authentic cultural identity as black or African people is truly a never-ending one. And when we think that we have won a significant battle in this sacred campaign and are tempted to rest on our laurels, there are always fifth columnists who creep out of the proverbial wood-work and try to undo the progress that we have made. A case in point is the on-going saga surrounding the recent designation of Barbados' capital city Bridgetown and its military garrison as a **World Heritage site** by the **United Nations Educational Scientific and Cultural Organization** (UNESCO).

I personally welcomed the fact that UNESCO had decided to include '**Bridgetown and its historic Garrison**' on the World Heritage site list, but I was also quick to caution Barbadians that if this development was not handled properly, it could have severely negative consequences for our young developing nation!

Almost from the very start we began to witness certain colonialist-mined elements in our society seeking to exploit UNESCO's recognition of Bridgetown's collection of colonial era buildings by using it as an opportunity to resurrect the old racist and colonialist conception of Barbadian history—the outdated version of our history that was based on the British and local white elites being placed at the centre of the historical narrative, and the masses of black Barbadians being treated as subsidiary objects of that history.

That racist, colonialist conception of our history was discredited and debunked as a result of the scholarly work of native Barbadian historians such as Woodville Marshall, Hilary Beckles, Kamau Brathwaite, Trevor Marshall, David Browne, Henderson Carter and Rodney Worrell, and the work of a long roster of individual activists and cultural organizations, inclusive of Elombe Mottley, Bobby Clarke, **Israel Lovell Foundation**, **Pinelands Creative Workshop**, and the **Clement Payne Movement**. However, the forces of backwardness and reaction are never completely defeated, and what we are now witnessing is a determined effort on their part to wage a counter-revolution, and to take us back to the bad old days of Barbados being conceived of as 'Little England'.

The best response to this type of counter-revolution is knowledge. And I would therefore like to urge all Barbadians to get intimately acquainted with the history of their country, and to allow that historical information to educate and instruct them. This, indeed, would be a sign of true national maturity.

Any proper understanding of the history of Barbados must begin with an acknowledgment that Barbados was, pre-eminently, the location of the first major industrial organization of the **Industrial Revolution**— the integrated sugar plantation and factory of the 17th and 18th centuries. It was the 17th and 18th century integrated sugar plantation and factory that produced the tremendous wealth on which both modern Britain and historic Bridgetown were developed.

But the full significance of this fact only sinks in when we recognize that the persons whose physical labour, intellectual ability, and technical capacities ran this complex and sophisticated precedent-setting industrial enterprise were our very own enslaved black Barbadian ancestors.

We tend to think of our enslaved forebears as mere manual labourers or perhaps even 'beasts of burden'. But nothing could be further from the truth. As the distinguished historian, Richard Pares, recorded in his book entitled *Merchants and Planters*:

> "With the mill, the boiling house and the still went an army of specialists, almost all of them slaves, but none the less specialists for that... and when we examine specifications of the Negroes we find so many boilers, masons, carters, boatswains of the mill, etc..."

The essential point is that the earliest industrial enterprise, which provided the initial capital upon which Europe's industrial civilization was built, was run—right here in Barbados—by a veritable army of black slave specialists. The Africans who were captured, reduced to slavery, and transported across the Atlantic ocean

15

to the Caribbean did not come empty-handed. Many of them came with sophisticated technical skills and knowledge acquired in their African homeland, and they all came with the intellectual ability to rapidly master the skills required to run the industrial economy that was emerging around them in islands like Barbados. And if we do not grasp those essential points we will not come to a proper understanding of our history and will be easy prey to the purveyors of the 'Little England' version of our history!

A correct knowledge of our history will also suggest to us that it is inappropriate to 'celebrate' the historic Garrison area—the historical home of Britain's largest and most important military facility in the Anglo-phone Caribbean.

The **Barbados Garrison** (also known as St. Ann's Garrison in honour of Britain's Queen Ann) was constructed by the British between 1705 and 1814 in order that it might be used as a military base for the British army. And the thousands of British soldiers stationed in Barbados were to be used for three specific missions— to maintain Britain's imperial rule of the West Indian territories; to put down rebellions by the enslaved blacks of Barbados and other British colonies; and to assist in attacking and destroying the independent nations and societies of West Africa, and imposing British colonial rule on Africa.

It was therefore the British imperial troops who called the Garrison their home, that were mainly responsible for putting down the **Bussa Rebellion** and killing the mighty General Bussa.

It was also these troops, in the form of the 2nd West India regiment, a regiment comprised of ex-slave black soldiers and white English officers, that were periodically shipped from their Garrison home base across the Atlantic to West Africa, where they wreaked havoc on the area of West Africa now known as Ghana, Gambia and Sierra Leone, burning and destroying towns and villages, and killing Africans who opposed British rule.

It is right that we acknowledge, come to terms with, and understand all aspects of our history. But there are some things that we just cannot celebrate.

Chapter 4

THE HURTFUL TRUTH ABOUT THE GARRISON

I HAVE said it before, and I will say it again: black people cannot and should not 'celebrate' the 'Garrison' (the collection of British military buildings on the outskirts of Bridgetown).

The Barbados government, the so-called cultural authorities, and the sundry professional and amateur historians who are exulting in UNESCO's designation of the Garrison as a world heritage site, and who are encouraging the Barbadian people to uncritically embrace and celebrate this physical edifice, are doing a tremendous disservice to our history, our ancestors, and to the current generation of Barbadians.

Yes, Barbadians need to know about the Garrison and its history. But what we need to know about the Garrison is its deep, complicated, hurtful and profound history; not the superficial, tourist brochure version of its history that our Government and its collaborators are currently promoting! For it is only by knowing and coming to terms with the hurtful truth of our history that Barbadians will mature as a people and develop genuine understanding and reconciliation among the racial groups that comprise our nation.

So, what place does the Garrison really occupy in the history of Barbados?

Well, first of all, the Garrison (properly known as '**St. Ann's Garrison**' in honour of Britain's Queen Ann), was one of the chief instruments utilized by our former British colonial masters to impose their colonialist and imperialistic domination on Barbados and the surrounding Caribbean territories.

The construction of the Garrison military complex began in 1705, when the British military authorities established St. Ann's Fort as a critical military facility to be used in their contest with France over the colonial domination and control of the Caribbean.

And then, in 1780, the British authorities decided to up the ante, and to establish a permanent Garrison in Barbados, centred around and incorporating St. Ann's Fort. This critical decision led to the construction, between 1789 and 1814, of the largest and most important British military base in the entire Caribbean—St. Ann's Garrison.

So let us be very clear. The Garrison and the thousands of white British soldiers who were stationed there played a central role in maintaining the evil system of 'chattel slavery' and in consolidating and defending Britain's colonial domination and exploitation of Barbados and the many other British colonies of the Caribbean. And so, when Barbadians are encouraged to admire the historic buildings of the Garrison, and to prance up and down around them, they must be given the information that will enable them to understand exactly what these buildings truly represent.

But there is another component of the Garrison story that is even more poignant and troubling. You see, the Garrison was used as the premier location for the enacting of one of the most profoundly evil psychological experiments ever inflicted on black or African people. I refer to the fact that the Garrison was the home base and training quarters of several British regiments comprised of formerly enslaved black or African soldiers, who were used to impose the system of slavery on their black kith and kin in the Caribbean, and to wreak death and destruction on their brothers and sisters in West Africa.

The Barbadians (black and white) who are being encouraged to celebrate the Garrison need to be told the tragic story of the predominantly black British West India regiments.

The idea that Britain should establish a number of black regiments was the brainchild of Lieutenant-General Sir John Vaughan, and was a response to the terrible death toll that tropical diseases and French soldiers were inflicting on white British troops in the Caribbean. In a December 1794 letter to the British Home Secretary, Lieutenant-General Vaughan stated as follows:

> "I am of the opinion that a corps of one thousand men composed of blacks and mulattoes, and commanded by British officers would render more essential service in the country, than treble the number of Europeans who are unaccustomed to the climate..."

And so was born the experiment of the West India regiment—an experiment that proved to be so successful for the maintenance of Britain's system of 'white supremacy' that, at its peak, no less than 12 British West India Regiments were brought into existence.

Imagine this scenario: several thousands of enslaved or formerly enslaved Africans, some of whom had fought for their freedom in North America—some of whom had been taken off of slave ships, some of whom had been purchased at slave auctions in Barbados and other slave colonies—railroaded into military service as black British soldiers commanded by white officers, and thousands of them being stationed at the Garrison in Barbados.

In the book entitled *The Empty Sleeve*, one of the most important explorations of the story of the West India regiments, the author Brian Dyde records that "the British Army became the biggest single purchaser of African slaves anywhere in the West Indies, and quite possibly anywhere throughout the Americas... At least thirteen thousand were bought during this period, from selected merchants who dealt with the owners and masters of slave ships."

The unfortunate and traumatized black man was given a freedom of sorts—the 'freedom' of a miserable, exploited, racially oppressed existence as a black British soldier. And the price that he had to pay for that 'freedom' was that he was obliged to use his strength and military skills to maintain the British system of slavery, and to assist Britain in carving out a colonial empire in West

Africa.

And so it was the black soldiers of the 1st West India Regiment who marched out of their barracks at the Garrison, and played the key military role in putting down the 1816 **Bussa slave rebellion** in Barbados. Bryan Dyde informs us in *The Empty Sleeve* that "Colonel Edward Codd, commander of St. Anne's Garrison, ordered the 1st West India Regiment under Major James Cassidy into the field... Just to the east of Bridgetown Cassidy came across a dense mob of half armed slaves crowning the summits of the low hills in Christ Church parish... the **1st West India Regiment** stormed the heights, and... drove the rebels from their position... the rebels had been led to believe by some of their leaders that troops of their own colour and ancestry would not be used against them..."

Thus, it was mainly black soldiers of the West India regiment who broke the back of the Bussa Rebellion, with the local white militia merely playing the lead role in the subsequent 'mopping up' operations. One can only imagine the horrific psychological turmoil that these black soldiers and rebels must have found themselves ensnared in.

The Garrison-based black soldiers of the 1st and 2nd West India regiments also found themselves pressed into service in a broad band of territory on the west coast of Africa that, today, constitutes the African nations of Ghana, Guinea, Sierra Leone and Gambia.

Between the years 1820 and 1896 the British military establishment regularly shipped battalions of the West

India regiments from their home bases in Barbados and Jamaica across the Atlantic ocean to assist in conquering and pacifying the indigenous nations and tribes of West Africa.

Black soldiers from the Garrison in Barbados, under the command of white officers, were required to attack and destroy towns and villages populated by their own African countrymen and women, and to help reduce to colonial servitude such proud African nations as the Ashanti of Ghana.

Let us go once again to *The Empty Sleeve* for the story of how in 1860, six companies of the Garrison-based 2nd West India Regiment punished and subdued the people of Badibu in present day Gambia:

> "The force moved inland on 17th February to the village of Kerewan, drove off some halfhearted defenders and burnt it to the ground before moving on to the town of Suwarracunda and repeating the exercise... Two more towns, Saba and Kinti Kunda had been destroyed by 20th February, and plans were made to attack a third... No sooner had Saba been reduced to ashes... messengers came... from the ruler of Jokadu, the small chiefdom to the west of Badibu... obviously concerned about the devastation and carnage taking place... he offered to mediate... the armistice was duly arranged and on 26th February a treaty was signed by the ruler of Badibu."

But perhaps a more graphic picture of the human cost

of the devastation that these Garrison-based soldiers wrought on West Africa is provided by a contemporary description of the 1883 destruction of the town of Talia in present day Sierra Leone:

> "Inside the town the sight was ghastly in the extreme. In a small space one officer counted eighty-two dead; in another part twenty-three bodies were lying huddled together, evidently the work of a single shell; and here and there were scattered groups of threes and fours, while a single corpse supported by a fence, stood up, grim in death..."

It would also be remiss of me to fail to mention that the black soldiers of the West India Regiments mutinied on three occasions: in 1801, the 8th WI Regiment, stationed at Fort Shirley in Dominica, staged a revolt that was put down by a white British regiment, resulting in 70 black soldiers killed or wounded and 7 sentenced to death; in 1808, the 2nd WI Regiment, stationed at Fort Augusta in Jamaica mutinied; and in 1837, the 1st WI Regiment commenced a revolt from their St. Joseph barracks in Trinidad, resulting in 40 black soldiers being killed in battle and 5 being sentenced to death. No mutiny ever took place at the Garrison in Barbados.

This, then, is a picture of the devilish, mind-numbing horror that the Garrison military facility represented for the black people of Barbados, the Caribbean and Africa in the 19th century. At the heart of it all was the phenomenon of Africans being organised and led by Europeans to inflict death and destruction on fellow Africans. Surely there is a profound message in this historical story for all Barbadians, but it seems to have totally escaped our governmental and cultural authorities.

Understand and come to terms with the history of the Garrison, we must. But celebrate and exult in it? Never!

Chapter 5

WILL THE REAL REVOLUTIONARIES STAND UP PLEASE?

IF there had been a CNN, a Fox News or a BBC three hundred and fifty years ago in 1652, Barbados would have been the leading international news story of the day. All over the world, people would have been talking about the remarkable news of the signing of the **Charter of Barbados** at Oistins Town by representatives of the Commonwealth or Republic of Great Britain and representatives of the citizens of a self-declared independent Barbados.

Journalists in all of the great centres of civilization in Africa, Europe and Asia would have been marvelling at the fact that a number of the inhabitants of the small British colony of Barbados had exhibited the audacity to unilaterally declare their independence from Great Britain on 18th February 1651, had gone on to fight a war of independence against Britain, and had finally been forced to capitulate to the much greater military might of Great Britain in January 1652, but on terms that did much honour to Barbados.

Freedom-loving people all over the world would have been thrilled to read the text of Barbados' declaration of

Independence:

> "Shall we be bound to the Government and Lordship of a Parliament in which we have no Representatives or persons chosen by us for there to propound and consent to what might be needful to us, as also to oppose and dispute all what should tend to our disadvantage and harm? In truth, this would be a slavery far exceeding all that the English nation hath yet suffered... So we will not alienate ourselves from those old heroic virtues of true English men, to prostitute our freedom and privileges to which we are born, to the will and opinion of any one; neither do we think our number so contemptible, nor our resolution so weak, to be forced or persuaded to so ignoble a submission, and we cannot think, that there are any amongst us who are so simple, and so unworthily minded, that they would not rather choose a noble death than forsake their old liberties and privileges."

Furthermore, all the political pundits of the day would have noted that the Charter of Barbados had established the fundamental political and economic principle of "no taxation without representation" when it stated: "No taxes, customs, imports, loans or excise shall be laid, nor levy made on any of the inhabitants of this island without their consent in a General Assembly." (Thus, Barbados had dealt with and resolved the fundamental issue around which the American Revolution was fought and won, a full 124 years before George Washington, Thomas Jefferson, Alexander Hamilton and the other American revolutionaries took up arms against Great Britain!)

And so, little Barbados would have been the talk of the day, with oppressed people all over the world marvelling at the thrilling words and sentiments of freedom emanating from the bold Barbadians.

But in the midst of all this excitement, the more thoughtful and sober analysts would have noted that underlying the seemingly stirring Barbados story lay some very harsh, dark and ignoble contradictions and realities.

Firstly, they would have been forced to recognise that the Barbadians who spoke and wrote so magnificently about "freedom" were all white men who had reduced tens of thousands of African men and women to slavery in Barbados, and a similar number of poor Europeans to indentured servitude!

Secondly, it would not have escaped them that the Barbadians were declaring Independence not so much of Britain, but of "Republican Britain!" You see, the Barbadians had declared Independence in the midst of the English Civil War, and at a time when the anti-Monarchy forces under Oliver Cromwell had defeated and executed the British King, and had declared Britain to be a Republic. The Barbadians were therefore repudiating the progressive political ideal of republicanism, and were wedding themselves to the backward and obsolete institution of the British monarchy.

Unfortunately therefore, these harsh contradictions and realities take much of the gloss off an episode in our Barbadian history that we would otherwise wish to celebrate. But if we are looking for a true and thrilling story of mid-17th century Barbadian revolutionism to celebrate, we don't have to look any further than the year 1649—arguably the most revolutionary year in the history of Barbados.

The year 1649 was the year in which both segments of the oppressed Barbadian working-class—the white indentured servants and the enslaved black Africans— erupted in separate gestures of revolt against the repressive white slave master class, the class of men who, one year later, would go on to issue the famous Barbadian version of a declaration of independence.

Several historians of 17th century Barbados record the plotting of a major insurrection by the white indentured servants of Barbados in 1649. Unfortunately the conspiracy was discovered and 18 of the principal poor white revolutionaries were executed. But such horrific 'exemplary punishment' did not deter a number of enslaved Africans from also plotting, in the said year of 1649, to revolt by setting fire to the plantation on which they were incarcerated. Sadly, this plot too was sold out, and the conspirators received what the historian, Richard Ligon, described as "condign punishment."

The fundamental point to be made therefore is that while the revolutionary activism of the wealthy white slave-owning Barbadians of 1652 is of great historical importance, yet it pales in comparison to the thoroughgoing, uncompromised revolutionism of the white indentured servants and enslaved Africans of Barbados who set out to overthrow an evil system of human oppression.

Barbadians need to spend much more time investigating and getting to know their own history—all of it—the good, the bad, the indifferent, the inspiring. For it is only by knowing our history and realistically accepting it for what it is, that we will develop a collective firmly rooted sense of Barbadian identity, and arrive at a place of greater racial understanding and acceptance of each other as fellow Barbadians.

Chapter 6

A BARBADIAN
PROFILE IN COURAGE

I WOULD like to share a truly outstanding example of Black courage and heroism drawn from the annals of Barbadian history.

It was the year 1675, and the oppressive British slave colony of Barbados was celebrating its 50th year of existence. By 1675 the island of Barbados had developed into the prized 'jewel' in the British 'crown' of colonial territories, and boasted a white population of 23,000 persons, and an enslaved black population of some 33,000 souls.

Furthermore, by 1675 the white slave-masters of Barbados had worked out a comprehensive system for keeping the enslaved Blacks or Africans in check and under control. According to the English writer, Richard Ligon, who published his *A True & Exact History of Barbadoes in 1657*, the slaveocracy's method consisted of the following three components:

(1)   the Blacks were rigorously prevented from coming into contact with any weapons whatsoever, while, of course, the Whites were well armed with muskets and other firearms;

    (2)   the Blacks were kept in a state of shock and
           awe by the fearsomeness, power and brutality
           of the slavery regime; and

    (3)   the enslaved Blacks were drawn from various
           regions of Africa, and as a result spoke
           different languages and therefore experienced
           difficulty in communicating with each other.

It was in this milieu that a network of enslaved Blacks or Africans, residing on several plantations across Barbados, spent three years meticulously hatching a plot to over-power and destroy the white slave-master class, and to take over control of the island.

This momentous event in the history of Barbados was recorded in a 1676 United Kingdom publication entitled *Great Newes from the Barbadoes*, or *A True and Faithful Account of the Grand Conspiracy of the Negroes*. The author recorded that the African-Barbadians had chosen "an ancient Gold Coast Negro" called 'Cuffy' to be crowned the new king of Barbados, and had designed an insurrection that was to commence with setting fire to the fields of sugar cane, and culminate in a general slaughter of the slave-masters.

Unfortunately for the network of revolutionaries, a female domestic slave by the name of Anna (alias Fortuna) overheard one of the rebels trying to persuade a reluctant teenager to join the plot. Anna spoke with the young slave, discovered that the uprising was due in two weeks' time, and persuaded the youth to go with her to inform her slave-master, Judge Gyles Hall.

Judge Hall, in turn, went in haste to the Governor, Sir Jonathan Atkins, and he immediately mobilised his corps of military guards to arrest the known conspirators. Governor Atkins also declared Martial Law, and within days more than one hundred African-Barbadian suspects had been arrested and subjected to a barbaric process of interrogation, torture, trial and execution.

Seventeen of the black suspects were immediately found guilty and sentenced to death, with six being burnt alive and eleven beheaded and dragged through the streets of Speightstown.

It was against this background of utter horror and barbarity that the shining, imperishable heroism of an African-Barbadian revolutionary hero known simply as ' Tony' emerged!

Tony, described by his captors as "a sturdy rogue, a Jew's Negro," was in the presence of another condemned rebel who was being prepared for death by burning. The 'Provost Marshall' or superintendent of security was in attendance, and he proceeded to urge this unfortunate man to confess and to name others before he died. The obviously terrorised black man responded by calling for water—a sign that he was prepared to speak and to divulge information.

Thereupon, Tony immediately spoke up and admonished him as follows: "Thou Fool, are there not enough of our Countrymen killed already? Art thou minded to kill them all?" This rebuke caused the condemned man to remain silent! And, in obvious resentment, one of the white spectators shouted to Tony:

"Tony, Sirrah, we shall see you fry bravely by and by!"

Tony's response to this threat of the most horrible death imaginable was to declare proudly and defiantly: "If you Roast me today, you cannot roast me tomorrow!" and to bid the executioner to proceed.

Tony was burnt to death, one of forty-two heroes who were executed for having the audacity to claim their freedom and dignity. Five others committed suicide in jail, while seventy were either deported or sent back to their so-called 'owners' after a savage flogging.

Tony's example, and his immortal cry of courage and defiance: "If you roast me today, you cannot roast me tomorrow!" should be remembered, honoured and cherished by every generation of Barbadians! What magnificent and exemplary courage, dignity, brotherhood and solidarity!

Our generation of Barbadians would do well to look back to that fateful year of 1675, and to adopt as our second national motto, a ringing cry with which to confront our enemies: "If you roast me today, you cannot roast me tomorrow!"

We wish to implore the Barbadians of this generation to be ever conscious of their great heritage, and to carry themselves with such dignity, courage and self-respect that they show themselves to be worthy sons and daughters of our magnificent 'Tony'.

Chapter 7

THE MAN WHO SHOULD HAVE BEEN KING OF BARBADOS

FORTY-SEVEN years after Barbados supposedly won its independence from the United Kingdom, we are still celebrating the Queen of England's birthday and nominating outstanding Barbadians for honours that are dispensed by this most English of queens on her birthday.

We Barbadians seem to be so devoted to this Caucasian queen, the leading representative of an institution that participated intimately in the enslavement and oppression of our ancestors, that we would seemingly do anything to continue clinging to her royal cloak-tails.

But perhaps the real source of this seeming devotion to Elizabeth II is an ingrained Barbadian regard for the institution of monarchy in general, rather than any particular love for the distant octogenarian who currently sits on the throne of England.

Well, if this is the case, perhaps Barbadians might be interested in exploring the story of the great black man who should have been King of Barbados—almost exactly 336 years ago.

It was the year of 1675, and the 50-year-old British

slave colony of Barbados had settled into a routine of importing large numbers of enslaved Africans from the Upper and Lower Guinea coasts of West Africa—the present day nations of Guinea, Sierra Leone, Liberia, Ivory Coast, Ghana, Togo, Benin and Nigeria—and working them to death on the island's burgeoning sugar plantations.

At the time, Barbados was firmly in the grip of an elite class of white plantocrats who, having survived the revolutionary year of 1649, the year in which both the white indentured servants and the black slaves made unsuccessful attempts at rebellion, were in a state of over-confident complacency about their dominance over the oppressed labouring class.

What the white Barbadian slave masters had failed to take proper note of was that increasingly, a much higher proportion of the newly imported enslaved Africans were so-called 'Coromantees' from the Gold Coast region of the Lower Guinea Coast—present day Ghana.

In Dr. Richard Allsop's *Dictionary of Caribbean English Usage* it is explained that 'Coromantee' was a "name used to identify a particular kind of slaves from the Gold Coast noted both for their sturdiness and fidelity on the one hand and for their fierce vengefulness when ill-treated."

Well, needless-to-say, it was not long before the tremendously ill-treated 'Coromantees' of Barbados decided to take matters into their own hands! Finding the travails and indignities of slavery to be unbearable, they hatched a plot to rid Barbados of the vile slave masters, and to establish a black monarchical system of government with a Gold Coast elder by the slave-name of ' Cuffy' to be elevated to the throne as King of Barbados.

The story of Cuffy (the man who would be King of Barbados) and of the slave rebellion of 1675 has come down to us via a 1676 pamphlet that was published in England under the title *Great Newes from the Barbadoes*, or *A True and Faithful Account of the Grand Conspiracy of the Negroes against the English*. The pamphlet records that a rebellion was plotted by many "Coromantee or Gold-Coast Negroes" over a period of years, in such secrecy that even the wives of the plotters were unaware of it. And the central role of 'King Cuffy' in the enterprise was explained as follows:

> "An ancient Gold-Cost (sic) Negro called Cuffy was chosen as King, and he was to be crowned on June 12, 1675, in a Chair of State exquisitively wrought and carved after their mode with bows and arrows to be likewise carried in State before his Majesty their intended King: trumpets to be made of elephants' teeth and gourdes were to be sounded on several hills to give notice of their general rising, with a full intention to fire the sugar-canes, and so run in and cut their masters, the Planters' throats in their respective Plantations..."

Unfortunately, the meticulously planned rebellion was sold out two weeks before the commencement date by a young 18-year-old slave who had lost his nerve. This led to Martial Law being declared by the governor— Governor Atkins—and to the conspirators being arrested *en masse.* A summary court of "oyer and terminer" was appointed to examine and try more than 100 suspects, and at the end of it all, some forty-two slaves were executed, five committed suicide in jail, and seventy were either deported or sent back to their owners after a savage flogging.

What, you may ask, became of "King Cuffy?" Well, no-one can say for certain, but it is likely that he was one of the executed martyrs. The truth is that we don't know a lot about Cuffy, the man who should have been King of Barbados, other than that he was African (Gold Coast) born, and was of advanced age.

In his definition of the word 'Coromantee', the late Dr. Allsopp goes on to tell us that the word was derived from the "name of a coastal Fante town... about 80 miles west of Accra" in modern day Ghana. So, in all likelihood, King Cuffy, like so many of his early fellow black Barbadians, belonged to the Fante ethnic group of modern day Ghana. The Fante speak the language known as 'Twi' and are a constituent ethnicity within the broad Eastern Akan culture system. They are therefore closely related to such ethnic groups as the Asante, Bron, Wassa and Denkyira.

Cuffy would have been brought to Barbados some time around the middle of the 17th century. And if we consult Volume V of UNESCO's *General History of Africa* we learn that around the beginning of the 17th century the Akan were a people who primarily lived in towns ruled by kings and queens, and in villages ruled by chiefs. Akan society was therefore a fairly evolved and sophisticated mechanism that had already become stratified with a ruling aristocracy consisting of priests and Kings, ordinary subjects, and a relatively small number of domestic serfs or slaves. Thus, Cuffy may very well have sprung from the ruling or aristocratic strata of his Fante town or village!

It is also interesting to speculate on what type of occupation Cuffy might have pursued in the Gold Coast. The Akan engaged in a wide variety of economic activities, including farming (plantain, bananas, yam and rice), collecting of kola nuts, livestock raising (poultry, sheep, goats and pigs), fishing, salt-making, textile weaving, gold-mining and last but no means least, trading. The Akan had long traded with the neighbouring Ewe and Ga people, with fish, salt, pottery, gold, chewing sticks, ivory, iron or metal wear being the main items of trade. They also carried on an external trade with the Western Sudan region, particularly during the heyday of the great Mande empire of Songhay in the 15th and 16th centuries.

And so, we know for certain that Cuffy came from a very sophisticated and industrious society, and he must therefore have found it very difficult to countenance the status that slave society sought to impose upon him in Barbados—the status of a soul-less thing, a chattel, a beast of burden, a hewer of wood and drawer of water in perpetuity.

This Akan King refused to accept any such slave status, and was willing to risk making the ultimate sacrifice in an heroic bid to destroy slavery and to establish some semblance of the Akan civilization right here in

Barbados!

All conscious Barbadians should therefore lift up and revere the name of Cuffy, the 'king-man' who our ancestors selected to be the true monarch of Barbados. Can any such claim be made for Queen Elizabeth II?

Chapter 8

THE INCONVENIENT TRUTH ABOUT WILBERFORCE

TWO hundred years ago, when the United Kingdom Parliament abolished the British trade in enslaved Africans, the English 'establishment' indulged in an 'orgy' of self-congratulations.

They positively wallowed in smug and sentimental self-satisfaction and declared to themselves and to the world at large that they were the most noble, humane and enlightened people in the history of civilization. For example, the then Bishop of London grandiloquently described the *Abolition Act* as "a great and signal act of humanity" which "would immortalize the British Senate and display to an admiring world the striking contrast between this country... the great stay and hope of the civilized world."

But in all their celebrations and self-praise it seemingly never occurred to them to take a little time out to engage in some critical self-examination or to make an effort at atonement for all the damage that they had done to the nations and peoples of Africa over a period of some 250 years. Instead of focusing on the untold millions of Africans that they had victimized—including the 1 million enslaved Africans that were still incarcerated on plantations in the British West Indian colonies in 1807—they were consumed with praising themselves and their alleged abolitionist leader, William Wilberforce.

One would have thought that with the benefit of 200 years of hindsight the British establishment in the year 2007 would have been able to recognize the immorality and folly of the behaviour of their 1807 forefathers and would have sought to make amends in their 2007 commemorations. Alas, this was not to be and the same moral deficiencies of 1807 were repeated in 2007. Once again, their focus was on self-praise, self-congratulations and the propagandistic eulogizing of William Wilberforce.

It is against this background therefore, that I propose to bring to public attention a few 'inconvenient truths' about Mr. William Wilberforce and his true role in the campaign to abolish the British slave trade and the system of racialised chattel slavery.

Let us begin by placing Wilberforce in context. After establishing and operating a British trade in enslaved Africans for more than 200 years, twelve Englishmen came together on 22nd May, 1787 to form a **Committee For The Abolition of The Slave Trade**. The twelve comprised Granville Sharp, Thomas Clarkson and ten members of the Quaker faith.

Two years later, in 1789, William Wilberforce, a wealthy 30-year-old Member of Parliament, agreed to join and assist the Committee. However, whilst Committee members like Thomas Clarkson took upon themselves the onerous and dangerous work of travelling the country, establishing sub-organizations and collecting evidence about the evils of the slave trade, Wilberforce basically confined his efforts to introducing once-a-year motions in the House of Commons calling for the abolition of the slave trade.

On 12th May 1789, Wilberforce rose in the House of Commons to make his first speech against the slave trade and revealed a pattern of thought that was to persist with him throughout his entire career. To begin with, Wilberforce attacked no one in Britain for the evils of the slave trade—certainly not the wealthy, conservative absentee planters with whom he shared a similar social background and social life, and not even the avaricious merchants and ship-owners who Wilberforce described as "men of humanity" in his speech. Rather, his harsh words of condemnation were reserved for "African chiefs and kings" whose "personal avarice and sensuality" he blamed for the maintenance of the slave trade.

Also characteristic was the manner in which the debate on Wilberforce's motion ended, with Wilberforce meekly agreeing that it be suspended until the House of Commons could carry out further investigations into the trade.

In the debate on his second motion on the slave trade, introduced in the Commons in 1791, Wilberforce turned with a vengeance on the people of Africa, declaring that "negroes are creatures like ourselves, but their minds are uninformed and their moral characters are debased... their state of civilization is very imperfect, their notions of morality extremely rude." He also used this speech to make it absolutely clear that in his opinion the enslaved Africans were not fit for freedom and that he was not asking for the abolition of slavery. And in a later speech he characterized Africans as "an ignorant, low, peevish, bloody and a thievish race". The only form of abolition that Wilberforce was prepared to contemplate was a gradual abolition in which freedom would come at some time in the distant future.

Also noteworthy about this phase in the abolitionist campaign was Wilberforce's refusal to support the so-called 'anti-saccharism movement' of the early 1790's—a popular boycott of slavery-made West Indian sugar. Wilberforce was so intent on distancing himself from anything that smacked of stirring up popular feeling that he declared the time was not right for a boycott.

And then the mighty 'Haitian Revolution' exploded in 1792, with armies of self-liberated blacks led by Toussaint L'Ouverture, Henry Christophe and Jean Jacques Dessalines dramatically wrenching the wealthy French colony from the hands of white enslavers and abolishing slavery in Haiti! This epoch-making event proved to be a 'litmus test' which literally separated the abolitionist boys from the abolitionist 'men' in Britain.

Reeling from public criticism that their anti-slave trade campaign would provoke a similar black uprising in the British West Indian colonies, Wilberforce and many of the other abolitionists went to great lengths to distance themselves from the Haitian Revolution and to emphasize that they had no intention of advocating the abolition of slavery.

When English troops invaded black ruled Haiti, Wilberforce rose up in Parliament to denounce a motion calling for the removal of the troops.

So extreme was the retreat from activism that in May 1794 the Abolition Committee (now known as the Abolition Society) gave up their rented offices. Subsequently, the Society met only occasionally in 1795 and 1796, and ceased meeting altogether in 1797 for an extended 7 year period.

Wilberforce, for his part, presented a watered down anti-slave trade bill in 1794, which was easily defeated. Several other bills he introduced in the mid 1790s suffered a similar fate, and Wilberforce eventually stopped introducing abolition bills altogether towards the end of the 1790s.

The American historian, Adam Hochschild, summed up Wilberforce's record as a Parliamentary advocate of abolition as follows: "Year after year, Wilberforce introduced an abolition bill, but he remained as poor a strategist as ever. He would propose the bill either too late in the legislative session or when MPs were distracted by some other issue, and he was too disorganized to muster his supporters."

When finally the British Parliament came to pass an abolition bill in 1807, it was not a bill introduced by Wilberforce that was debated. Rather, it was the governing administration of Lord Grenville that introduced the slave trade abolition bill as the official policy of the British government. And significantly, when during that 1807 Parliamentary debate, a young

Member of Parliament proposed that all infants born to slaves henceforth be free, Wilberforce opposed this idea.

Wilberforce also famously denounced the British Government for prohibiting the whipping of enslaved women, and it was he who first introduced the notion that in the event that slavery was abolished, the white slave owners should be compensated for their loss of property. It is not surprising therefore that a couple years after Wilberforce's death in 1833, Thomas Clarkson commented that Wilberforce "cared nothing about the slaves, nor if they were all damned, provided he saved his soul."

Yet another abolitionist, George Stephen, characterized Wilberforce as a man of "busy indolence" who "worked out nothing for himself" and who felt "too much deferential regard for rank and power."

But perhaps the most incisive critique of Wilberforce came from the radical female abolitionist of the period, Elizabeth Coltman, who noted that "so long as it was maintained that the slave was not fit for freedom, he would remain a slave, since it was the system itself which prevented him from ever being 'fit' for anything but slavery... To say, therefore, as did Wilberforce that the slaves had to remain slaves until they were fit to be free was condemning them to perpetual bondage."

The hard historical facts clearly establish that Wilberforce was no 'friend' or 'brother' of the African, enslaved or free. Wilberforce was first and last, a socially conservative churchman who belonged to the so-called 'Evangelical' wing of the Anglican Church, and who was driven by the idea of elevating the morals and manners of what he considered to be depraved elements of his beloved England, thereby saving the soul of his nation from a harsh judgment by Divine Providence. As a result, Wilberforce was capable of despising Africans and supporting their continued enslavement, while at the same time trying to save his nation from the eternal judgment which, in his religious imagination, the obvious evils of the slave trade would call forth. These contradictions resulted in Wilberforce's abolitionism being half-hearted and ineffectual.

It should be noted as well that Wilberforce's severely limited **abolitionism** was but one component of a cluttered agenda of bourgeois moral and social reformism. His career was actually devoted to self-righteous agitation against those he considered to be "lukewarm Christians" and against such "transgressions" as sensuality, swearing, drinking, fornication and **Sabbath-breaking**. In addition, as a socially conservative Parliamentarian he supported virtually all of the repressive measures of his era, including a law that provided 3-month jail terms for anything remotely resembling labour organizing, an activity which he considered to be "a general disease in our society." He also trenchantly denounced the idea of women being permitted to play any role in the abolition movement.

So it would be totally wrong to credit Wilberforce with having made "a magnificent contribution" to the abolition of the British slave trade, much less to the abolition of slavery itself. The reality is that the abolition of the

British trade in enslaved Africans was precipitated by the drastic decline in wealth and importance to Britain of the West Indian colonies; the coming on stream of both the Industrial Revolution and the British Empire of the East and the incessant slave rebellions which constantly portended the likelihood of "abolition from below" by the slaves themselves.

One can legitimately charge Wilberforce with setting in place trends which led to untold grief for African people from the mid 19th century up to today. You see, Wilberforce made respectable the notions of 'White Superiority' and the alleged 'white man's burden' to bring 'civilization' to what he considered to be ignorant and benighted Africans through the imperialist carving up and colonization of the African continent. There is therefore a direct line between Wilberforce's brand of racist, paternalistic abolitionism and later British imperialism and colonization in Africa.

If indeed we are looking for historical personalities who made 'magnificent contributions' to the abolition of the slave trade and slavery itself, it would make much more sense to look to our own black revolutionaries, most of whom actually gave their lives in the armed struggle to end slavery. Rather than singing undeserved praises to Wilberforce, let us instead lift up the names of Tacky, Nanny and Sam Sharpe of Jamaica, Cuffy and Quamina of Guyana, Balla and Pharcell of Dominica, Chatoyer and Duvalle of St. Vincent, Bussa, Nanny Gregg and Washington Franklin of Barbados, Daaga of Trinidad, Fedon of Grenada and of course the magnificent 'Black

Jacobins' of Haiti.

Chapter 9

THE SLAVES WHO
ABOLISHED SLAVERY

WHO or what was ultimately responsible for the abolition, in 1834, of the British system of 'racialised' chattel slavery?

The great Caribbean historian, Dr. Eric Williams, identified five sets of factors that ultimately brought down the system that, over 300 years, had been responsible for the enslavement and murders of tens of millions of Africans.

First of all, he pinpointed economic factors. Put simply, the 'triangular trade' and the slave-run West Indian colonies had lost their former importance to the British economy and had therefore become expendable.

Dr. Williams also cited political factors in his epic study, *From Columbus to Castro*. He was of the view that the abolition of the Caribbean slave system was part and parcel of the general, and eventually successful, struggle of the rising industrial bourgeoisie against the landed aristocracy in Britain.

Williams also gave some limited credit to both the humanitarian agitation engaged in by such European abolitionists as Clarkson, Wilberforce and Buxton in England, and Victor Schoelcher in France, and to complex considerations of intra-European colonial rivalry which motivated and drove the policy of the British Government.

But it is the fifth factor identified by Williams that I wish to focus on in this chapter—the hundreds of thousands of enslaved Africans of the British West Indies and their record of persistent and unstoppable rebellion.

The American historian, Michael Craton, author of the book entitled *Testing The Chains*, has identified no less than 75 slave plots and rebellions in the British West Indies in the 200 year span between 1638, the beginning phase of British slavery in the West Indies, and 1838, the year in which the slavery system finally collapsed in the British colonies.

The record in our own little colony of Barbados is as follows:

> **1649**: a servile revolt involving slaves as well as white indentured servants
>
> **1675**: a 'Coromantee' plot led by enslaved Africans known as Tony and Cuffee, and betrayed by a 'house negress' called Anna Fortuna
>
> **1683**: a plot involving mainly Africa born slaves
>
> **1686**: another major plot involving hundreds of mainly Africa born slaves
>
> **1692**: an Afro-creole plot led by Barbados

born enslaved Africans known as Ben, Sambo, Hammon and Sampson—all elite artisans—and once again betrayed by a slave informant.

1701: another major Afro-creole plot involving hundreds of conspirators

1816: the so-called **Bussa Rebellion** which was centered in St. Philip parish but which engulfed half the island and produced such heroes as Nanny Gregg, Jacky, Cain Davis, Joseph Pitt Washington Franklin, and of course General Bussa.

These and other rebellions produced outstanding and legendary examples of courage and determination. There was, for example, the case of one of the leaders of the 1675 Barbados plot, who, on the verge of being executed by burning, not only refused to reveal the names of his fellow conspirators, but defiantly shouted at his oppressors: "If you roast me today, you cannot roast me tomorrow!" and urged his executioner to proceed.

The Bussa Rebellion of 1816, the first of the 'great' 19th century slave rebellions in the British West Indies, sent such a forceful message of uncompromising hostility to slavery that in 1819, a full three years after the Rebellion, the Governor of Barbados, Lord Combermere, was still writing to the English Colonial Office warning them that "the public mind (in 'white' Barbados) is ever tremblingly alive to the dangers of insurrection."

This oppressive and formidable fear of a climactic

Black rebellion was not unique to Barbados. Dr. Eric Williams explained in *From Columbus To Castro* that "a Negro revolt in the British West Indies in the early 19th century, designed to abolish slavery from below, was widely apprehended, both in the West Indies and in Britain… In the British West Indies, it was no longer a question of slave rebellions if, but slave rebellions unless emancipation was decreed."

This assessment of the situation was borne out by Daniel O'Connell, the Irish leader in the British House of Commons who, in 1832, declared in Parliament that "the planter was sitting… over a powder magazine, from which he would not go away, and he was hourly afraid that the slave would apply a torch to it."

It is not surprising therefore that when Earl Stanley, the Secretary of State for the colonies, came to introduce the *Emancipation Act* in the British Parliament, he expressed the view that "they were compelled to act; for they felt that take what course they might, it could not be attended with greater evil than any attempt to uphold the existing state of things."

Thus, it was really the enslaved Africans themselves who, in the final analysis, were ultimately responsible for the abolition of slavery.

The critical factor was their relentless and implacable resistance!

And so it is right and fitting that we record and honour the tremendous contributions made to the cause of freedom by these heroic revolutionary fighters against slavery. Constraint of space does not permit us to note all 75 rebellions and plots; but a short list of some of the most outstanding examples is as follows:

1638: a Christmas-time rebellion on the island of Providence, involving hundreds of slaves

1690: a slave uprising in St. Kitts to coincide with a French invasion of the island

1730: the first Maroon War in Jamaica, involving Cudjoe, Nanny, and many other leaders

1735: island-wide Afro-creole plot in Antigua, led by Tacky and Tomboy

1760: Tacky's massive slave rebellion in Jamaica

1763: Cuffee's rebellion in Dutch Berbice (present day Guyana)

1769: Chatoyer's first Carib War in St. Vincent

1785: first Maroon War in Dominica led by Balla and Pharcell

1795: Fedon's Rebellion in Grenada

1796: the so-called "Brigands' War" in St. Lucia, involving many slaves

1823: massive rebellion in Demerara (present

day Guyana) led by Quamina and many others

1831: the so-called "Baptists War" in Jamaica, led by Deacon Sam Sharpe.

In the words of the Jamaican historian and statesman, Richard Hart, these were the "slaves who abolished slavery." And we, their children and beneficiaries, must never forget their names.

Chapter 10

REPARATIONS (I)

RECENTLY, there has been a lot of talk about 'Reparations!'

Some are saying that reparations are owed to Black or African people and nations and that the achievement of reparations is a path out of the debt, unemployment and poverty that plague so many of our people.

However, other persons maintain that it is impractical to pursue reparations and that the campaign for reparations will only sow racial bitterness and discord. Clearly, a lot of confusion surrounds the issue of reparations.

This article is therefore designed to remove some of this confusion, and to bring greater clarity to this critical issue.

First of all, let us establish what reparations is not. It is not about individual 'white' or European people making monetary payments to 'black' or African individuals. Reparations is not about revenge. It is not about holding the current generation of Whites or Europeans liable for the sins or crimes of their ancestors.

Reparations is not a Barbadian or even a Caribbean issue. It is an issue that extends way beyond Barbados and is being pursued by numerous nongovernmental organizations, and literally dozens of African, Caribbean and Latin America governments. Indeed, it was perhaps the central issue of the historic **United Nations' World Conference Against Racism** that was held in 2001.

Reparations is not a black or African issue. Reparations has been a Jewish issue, a Japanese-American issue, a Korean issue, an Aborigine issue, and most definitely a European issue.

The notion underlying the concept of reparations is that of repairing the damage caused to a nation or group of people.

Our first contact with the notion of reparations in Barbados occurred in 1834, when white Barbadian planters demanded and were paid financial compensation for the loss of what they considered to be their human '**property**' occasioned by the abolition of slavery.

The British government actually paid the slave-owners of the British West Indies the sum of £20 million as compensation for the loss of their 'human property'. Unfortunately, no one thought of compensating the enslaved Africans for their unpaid labour!

It is also noteworthy that the embattled and impoverished black Caribbean state of Haiti was required to pay millions of francs to the Government of France as reparation for the loss of 'property' suffered by France when Haitian slaves declared their freedom and independence.

Of course, these are warped and distorted uses of the concept of reparations, but they do demonstrate that the concept is not a new one, nor one that is foreign to Europeans.

However, throughout history, there have been many proper and legitimate uses of the instrument of reparations to bring justice and restitution to a variety of nations and people who have suffered historical wrongs.

When we examine this historical record, however, it becomes clear that there is one monumental historical wrong that has not yet been addressed, and that is crying out for justice and reparation. I refer to what must be considered to be the greatest holocaust in history, the 400-year-long syndrome of the mass kidnapping, enslavement and racist oppression of the people of Africa and their 'new world' progeny.

When Europe came face to face with Africa in the mid-15th century, Europeans found African nations and peoples which were on the same level of material development as the nations and peoples of Europe.

However, after 400 years of an European organized and controlled slave trade, and the plundering of Africa's human and natural resources, we now inhabit a world in which a tremendous material gap has been established between Europe and Africa, and between the sons and daughters of Europe and Africa in the new world.

Reparations is all about repairing the damage that has been done to Africa and its sons and daughters, and restoring some semblance of balance, equity and justice to world civilization.

Chapter 11

REPARATIONS (II)

VIRTUALLY all black nations that experienced slavery and colonialism find themselves today in a seemingly bottomless pit of debt, poverty, technological backwardness and unequal trade relations. For example in 1992, the total foreign debt of all Sub-Saharan African countries was estimated at $300 billion, a figure equivalent to 90 per cent of their combined Gross National Products. And in the year 2014, we in Barbados now labour under an approximate eight billion dollar national debt: a sum almost equivalent to our entire Gross National Product.

With 10 per cent of the world's population, Africa's share in world exports is a mere 1.4 per cent. In addition, the European-dominated international market grossly undervalues the prices of Africa's primary commodities, while every effort continues to be made to limit Africa's participation in manufacturing industry.

Furthermore all former slave colonies continue to be afflicted with widespread poverty. Even in Barbados, the highest placed Black nation on the UNDP's *Quality of Life Index*, it was estimated a few years ago that some 25,000 people exist on less than $25 per week. And yet another striking characteristic is that Black Africa's poverty problem is compounded by the fact that every year tens of billions of dollars are remitted from these countries to Europe and North America.

It is clear therefore that we are all in an extremely serious predicament, the causes of which were brilliantly laid bare by Dr. Walter Rodney in his book *How Europe Underdeveloped Africa*. Rodney explained that during the centuries of slavery and colonialism a monumental rape of the resources of Africa and its people was perpetrated, and European controlled structures were so firmly put in place that they continue to be used to plunder the resources of black people today.

If the people of Africa and the African Diaspora are to move forward there must be a fundamental restructuring of the international economic system. There must be wide-spread foreign debt cancellation, massive technology transfers from North to South, substantial capital inflows from Europe and North America, reconstruction of the major international economic and political institutions in order to make room for African decision-making power, and a reversal of our ever worsening terms of trade.

Back in the 1970s the countries of the Third World came together and made a collective demand for such revolutionary international reform. The complex of reform demands was known as the **New International Economic Order**, and most of them are to be found in Resolutions 3201 and 3202 of the UN General Assembly.

Tragically, the governments of the countries of Europe

and North America derailed the Third World movement for a New International Economic Order by deriding the effort as an exercise in begging for charity. The attitude of northern Governments was that they did not owe the people of the Third World anything.

We in the Reparations Movement wish to serve notice that the progressive Pan-Africanist forces throughout the African World have re-launched the movement for a New International Economic Order!

However, our Movement differs significantly from the Third World Movement of the 1970s. Rather than appealing to the non-existent conscience of the oligarchs of the white world, we are basing our demands on the concept of 'Reparations For The Crimes of Slavery And Colonialism'.

Slavery was a crime against humanity—a crime recognized in international law. As a matter of international law, the nations and institutions that profited from that crime must compensate the victims. They owe us!

Chapter 12

AFRICAN CIVILIZATION

WE cannot talk seriously about issues such as Slavery and Reparations without having a proper understanding of the inter-linked concepts of African Civilization and Pan-Africanism, and their relevance to us as a people.

How many times have we heard and witnessed jet black Barbadians, Jamaicans, Vincentians or Trinidadians declaring with passion that "I am not African!"

What is so ironic about this is that 150 years ago, the great grandparents of these same 'Caribbean people' harboured no doubts about their racial identity when they established 'back-to-Africa' movements and embraced such explicitly African organisations as the **African Methodist Episcopal Church**.

But the 'White World' has promulgated such a negative image of Africa with their Tarzan movies and CNN and BBC 'news' reporting, that many people of the African Diaspora routinely repudiate their African-ness.

This is a great tragedy, because as Malcolm X warned, "you can't love the fruit if you hate the tree!" In other words, if African Diasporans hate and repudiate Africa, they will inevitably hate and repudiate themselves, for in their heart of hearts they know that they are descendants of Africa!

So for our very own psychological health, if for nothing else, it is important that we combat the racist conspiracy to denigrate and marginalize Africa and to write Africa out of history. It is important that we take to heart the admonition of the great Caribbean poet, Martin Carter, and escape from the old 'nigger yard' of scorn and self hatred, and embrace a new psychology of self knowledge and self affirmation. It is time that we develop a proper understanding of the seminal and indispensable role that Africa and African people have played in the history of the world.

If we look at an accurate map of the world, not the conventional Eurocentric 'Mercator' projection map that illegitimately places Europe at the centre of the world and contracts the size of Africa and Asia, but the more modern 'Pieters' projection map, we will notice that the massive 12 million square mile African continent is truly the central land mass of planet Earth. Furthermore, if we do a little historical research we will discover that Africa was the birth place of humanity and the original home of human civilization.

It is accepted wisdom in the domains of anthropology and archaeology that the basic creatures which many scientists believe gave rise to both the apes and 'man' first emerged on the African continent during the 'Oligocene' age some 30 to 40 million years ago.

Africa also first saw the emergence of man-like creatures or hominids, variously named *Homo habilis, Homo erectus, Australopithecus africanus* and

Neanderthals, some 5 to 3 million years ago.

And of course the momentous development upon which the whole of human history is based occurred in Africa 150,000 years ago with the emergence of *Homo sapiens*, 'man' as we know him today, in the Great Lakes region (Uganda, Kenya, Tanzania, Rwanda) of Africa. Thus, whether one believes in evolution or creationism, the continent of Africa is central to the birth of mankind.

Having been born in the sunny climes of Africa, the original *Homo sapiens* were equipped with 'melanin' and a dark skin pigmentation to protect against the strong and ever present sunlight and its propensity to create vitamin D in the human body. And this is why we can confidently assert that the original 'man' was the black man.

The original African man began moving out of Africa some 40,000 years ago into colder areas of the earth that came to be known as Asia and Europe, and commenced a process of bodily adaptation to new and different physical environments which eventually produced the various so-called 'races' of mankind.

But once again, it was on the original mother continent of Africa that man's fundamental cultural breakthrough came in the form of the domestication of plants and animals approximately 17,000 years ago.

Thus, it was in Africa that men first moved beyond the migrant lifestyles associated with hunting and gathering and settled into stationary villages and permanent agricultural systems.

This was an era in which Africa with its settled,

agricultural based ethos was well in advance of Europe and much of the Asian steppe regions of the earth, which were still experiencing the end stages of a period of glaciation and were still characterized by nomadic patterns of human existence based on hunting, gathering and the herding of migratory flocks of animals.

It is important to emphasize the extent to which these two very different physical environments produced two very different culture systems. The American historian, William McNeil, explained this phenomenon as follows:

> "Pastoralists, like hunters, were parasites upon herbivores. They were like hunters, too, in pursuing a wandering life, moving comparatively large distances in search of grass for their animals... Above all else, shepherds and herdsmen had to protect their herds from rival carnivores, whether those rivals were animals or other men... **Warlike organization and habits of violence... remained near the surface of such a life, whereas the earliest farming communities were remarkably peaceable and egalitarian...** The subsequent history of mankind in the Old World turned upon an interplay between the superior numbers made possible by farming and the superior politico-military organization required by pastoralism. This balance tipped sometimes in favour of one side, sometimes in favour of the other, depending on ups and downs of social organization and cohesion, and on developments in technology."

What is clear, however, is that it was the warm

agriculture based, Africa-centred, 'Southern Cradle' of mankind that invented and gave birth to civilization'—a state of human society marked by a high level of intellectual, technological, cultural and social development.

The 'Southern Cradle' farming communities produced the earliest technological breakthroughs in the form of the plough, the lever, the wheel and axle, simple machines, techniques of irrigation, stone masonry and similar inventions, eventually coalescing into the world's first civilization, the Nile Valley civilization of Africa.

The high point of the Nile Valley culture system was the civilization of 'Kemet' or Egypt, but Kemet was preceded by earlier Nile Valley civilized cultures such as the Kingdom of 'Ta-Seti'.

Kemet proved to be so central to the cultural development of mankind, that it behooves us to spend some time reflecting on this great African civilisation. Initially divided into two competing kingdoms, the kingdoms of lower and upper Kemet, the classical 'Phaoronic' civilization of Kemet became firmly established around 3,200 B.C., when King Menes or Narmer unified the two kingdoms and established himself as Pharoah. Thus began the period of Man's highest cultural achievement, not only in the Nile Valley of Africa, but also in such satellite black or 'African' civilizations as 'Sumer' (present day Iraq) and 'Indus Valley' (present day India).

Our ancient Kemitic ancestors established the foundations of astronomy, mathematics, architecture, metallurgy, chemistry and medicine, and developed the principles of ethics, governance and religion to an extremely high level.

Tangible evidence of their achievement is to be found in the awe-inspiring pyramids of Giza; the almost universal acceptance of the spiritual concepts of monotheism and a universal God; the notion underpinning science that there are exact laws which order the universe; concepts of atomic structure and transmutation of elements; alphabet systems; and the concept of the territorial 'nation' state.

The classical African 'mentality' or 'personality' that took shape in the Nile Valley stressed the values of 'Ma'at'—peace, justice, harmony and goodness, over the values of war, and became centred on the worship of a universal God of transcendent moral values. Also central to classical African civilization were concepts of 'matriarchy' and 'social collectivism' which stressed the emancipation of women and a belief in the values of social duty and solidarity, and which were centred in the institution of the extended family.

The typical citizen of Kemet possessed a deep conviction that man was made in the likeness and image of God, and was therefore imbued with a sacredness or divine potentiality. He had no conception of European notions of 'original sin and guilt', and was convinced that there was a divine element or spirit that infuses both man and matter. It was commonly accepted that there are principles of nature which have been constructed by a higher intelligence which govern the universe and human and natural life, and that man possesses a special (divine) cognitive gift that allows him to discover these preexisting principles.

Nile Valley civilization was the high point of the black man's civilization—a towering human achievement that blazed the trail for humankind's cultural development over several thousand years.

Eventually, however, the territorial state of Kemet was brought down by the combined effects of internal decay, barbarian invasion (Assyrians, Persians, Greeks and Romans) and negative climatic and environmental changes.

But so powerful was its influence that for many centuries afterwards its magnificent culture and spirit was still being reflected in lesser successor civilizations throughout Africa. I refer to such important civilizations of the first 1,500 years of the 'Christian Era' as Kush or Nubia, Aksum, Ghana, Mali, Songhai and Monomotapa among others.

Yes, the centuries long European orchestrated 'Maafa' or 'Holocaust' of the Trans-Atlantic slave trade, chattel slavery and colonialism, did tremendous damage to the civilization of the entire African continent, but we must never allow them to foist in our minds the utterly false and evil notion that Africa is or was a continent of backwardness and lack of achievement. Nothing could be further from the truth!

Chapter 13

LONG LIVE THE
PAN-AFRICAN MOVEMENT

PAN AFRICANISM was born out of the severe oppression and anti-black racism that was visited upon the scattered sons and daughters of Africa during the centuries of European-imposed slavery and colonialism.

At one stage it became clear that all black or African descended people, whether they lived on the continent of Africa or in the Diaspora, faced a common predicament and therefore had a common interest in uniting with each other in an effort to emancipate themselves and rebuild their African civilization. The appellation applied to this noble sentiment and accompanying programme of action was the term 'Pan-African'.

Pan-Africanism is therefore both a philosophy and an organized people's movement. Put simply, it is a political and cultural phenomenon in which the continent of Africa, Africans, and African descendants outside of the continent are regarded as one unit. Pan-Africanism seeks to regenerate and unify Africa, and to promote a feeling of 'one-ness' among the people of the African World. In addition, it valorizes the African past, inculcates pride in African values, and seeks to organize the people of Africa and the Diaspora for the attainment of power and influence in the world.

Who was the initiator or creator of Pan-Africanism? Many of us might be surprised to learn that the credit for creating Pan-Africanism could well go to Barbados, and to a sadly neglected Barbadian hero by the name of Prince Hall.

Some of the historians of Pan-Africanism have traced its genesis to a 1787 petition that the African Lodge of Boston, under Grand Master Prince Hall, sent to the Legislative Assembly of the state of Massachusetts in the United States of America, requesting assistance for free Blacks who wished to return to Africa in order to rebuild their fortunes and the civilization of their ancestral continent.

Prince Hall is reputed to have been born on September 12, 1737 in Bridgetown, Barbados to an English father and a free coloured mother. At age 30 he left Barbados and migrated to the city of Boston in the United States where he continued his intellectual and social development. He was one of the most formidable opponents of slavery, and was an indomitable champion of American independence and civil and human rights for black men and women. Prince Hall can therefore be justifiably regarded as the 'father' of Pan-Africanism.

However, Prince Hall never used the word 'Pan-African' to describe his activities or his organization. We may therefore regard him as being Pan-Africanist in spirit and substance, even though not in name!

And a similar claim can be made for Edward Wilmot Blyden, the great 19th century West Indian-born

African intellectual and statesman who developed and promulgated a comprehensive Africanist philosophy based on the concepts of repatriation to Africa, the belief in the existence of a distinct 'African Personality' and a glorious African history of achievement, the need for a major national centre for the entire African race on the continent of Africa, and an almost religious belief in a coming grand African future.

Blyden was born in 1832 on the then Danish West Indian island of St. Thomas, and migrated to Liberia where he rose to great heights as a journalist, minister of religion, diplomat, scholar, writer and defender of the African cause. Like Prince Hall he too did not deploy or use the term 'Pan-Africanism'.

The term 'Pan Africanism' was initially coined by the Trinidadian, Henry Sylvester Williams, who organized the first self-styled 'Pan-African Congress' in the City of London, in the year 1900. This gathering of Caribbean and African-American intellectuals discussed the worldwide predicament of black people and petitioned the European powers for improved conditions and respect for the civil rights of Africans within the various European empires.

However, as important as this inaugural Pan African Congress was, we have to concede that it contained a number of weaknesses which were to manifest themselves in the three following congresses organized by the African-American scholar, W.E.B. Du Bois—they were meetings of individuals rather than organizations, they lacked the involvement of continental Africans and of representatives of the working masses, and they adopted the tactic of petitioning for limited goals rather than demanding African independence and organising African people to fight for this fundamental objective.

The Jamaican, Marcus Mosiah Garvey, came to the rescue and took the concept of Pan-Africanism to a higher level when he created a mass organization of some six million African people known as the Universal Negro Improvement Association (UNIA).

Garvey consciously committed himself to the attainment of 'Black Power' and African independence, and the U.N.I.A.'s historic 1920 Convention at Madison Square Garden in New York city brought together 25,000 Garveyites, a significant number of whom had come directly from the African continent. The Garvey mass movement constituted such a threat to the European powers that it was viciously attacked and subverted. Sadly, many of Garvey's goals were unrealized. However, Garvey had given the Pan-African Movement a profound vision that would lead it onwards to higher levels of achievement.

And those higher levels of achievement were not long in coming. In 1945, a number of the stalwarts of Pan-Africanism used the end of the Second World War as an opportunity to organize the fifth major Pan African Congress as a mechanism for building on the earlier work of Du Bois and Garvey.

The 1945 Pan-African Congress, held in Manchester, England, was principally organized by Kwame N'Krumah of Ghana, and by C.L.R. James and George

Padmore of Trinidad. This congress brought together the representatives of African and West Indian trade unions, political parties, and students' and civil rights organisations. These Pan-Africanists developed a practical, militant programme of struggle, and demanded the immediate independence of the African and West Indian colonies.

In addition, a permanent organization was set up, and the various participants returned to their home territories to carry on the struggle. And, needless-to-say, their strenuous efforts culminated in spectacular success! Indeed, by 1957 Kwame N'Krumah had achieved the independence of Ghana, and within the next 10 years, almost the entire African continent was formally decolonised!

The next stage in the development of Pan-Africanism saw the leaders of independent African countries meeting together in Addis Ababa, Ethiopia, and founding the Organization of African Unity (OAU) on the 25th of May 1963. The driving forces behind this critical development were President Kwame N'Krumah of Ghana and Emperor Haile Selassie of Ethiopia. And henceforth, the 25th of May was celebrated annually as African Liberation Day.

To its credit, the OAU went on to play a very important role in ensuring that the entire African continent was formally decolonized, and that the evil racist system of apartheid was eradicated—two missions that were brought to completion when the African National Congress came to power in South Africa's first democratic elections in 1994.

Subsequent to these heady achievements the leadership of the African continent came to the conclusion that the new age required a new type of Pan-Africanist organisation—one that would put a greater emphasis on economic integration and development, and that would include representatives of the African Diaspora in a much more fundamental manner than was the case with the OAU.

As a result, under the guidance of the late President Muammar Qaddafi of Libya, a decision was made in 1999 to disband the OAU, and to replace it with a new African Union (AU). The AU was inaugurated in Durban, South Africa in 2002. Its headquarters is located at Addis Ababa in Ethiopia, and it has distinguished itself by initiating a 'Diaspora Initiative' that conceptualises the Diaspora as a region of the African continent, and that is seeking to include formal representatives of the Diaspora in several of the organs of the AU.

Long live the glorious Pan-African Movement—in spirit and in substance!

Chapter 14

THE BARBADIAN TRADITION OF PAN-AFRICANISM

THE Barbadian tradition of Pan-Africanism that was started by Prince Hall in 1787 has been developed by a host of other outstanding Barbadian 'freedom fighters' over the past two centuries. I refer to such personalities as Bussa's 1816 revolutionaries (many of whom were transported to Sierra Leone after the military defeat of the Bussa Rebellion), the many 19th century Barbadian 'back-to-Africa' pioneers who played critical roles in developing Liberia, Sierra Leone, Gambia and Guinea, and such 20th century stalwarts as Richard B. Moore, John Beckles, Charles Duncan O'Neale, Israel Lovell, Reginald Pierrepoint, Clement Payne, Wynter Crawford and Leroy Harewood, among others.

But let us spend some time reflecting on what must be considered to be the single most remarkable Barbadian contribution to Pan Africanism—the 19th century 'back-to-Africa' repatriation of hundreds (if not thousands) of Barbadians, and the role that they played in the development of the West African nation of Liberia.

How many Barbadians are aware that almost immediately after the termination of slavery in 1838, many African-Barbadians formed and joined such 'back-to-Africa' organizations as the Barbados-based **African Colonisation Society**, with a view to returning permanently to their ancestral homeland? How many of us are aware that the black Barbadians of the mid-19th century consciously saw themselves as Africans?

The territory in Africa that proved most magnetic to these early Barbadian Pan-Africanists was Liberia. Initially established by the American Colonization Society on the west coast of Africa in 1820 as a 'free state' for formerly enslaved Africans, Liberia rapidly evolved into the independent black Republic of Liberia.

The major black Barbadian incursion into Liberia occurred in 1865, when, as a result of years of organization and preparation by such leading African-Barbadian citizens as London Bourne, Samuel Jackman Prescod, James Wiles and Anthony Barclay, some 346 Barbadians boarded a ship called *The Cora* at Bridgetown, and landed at Monrovia, the capital of Liberia, on 10th of May 1865. The Barbadians quickly established a totally new community known as **Crozierville**, and with the help of continuing infusions of capital and immigrants from Barbados in the years following, were able to make a tremendous impact on Liberian society.

Among the initial group of Barbadian migrants were Anthony Barclay, his wife Sarah Ann Barclay (the daughter of London Bourne) and their eleven children, including a 12 year old boy by the name of Arthur Barclay.

Tragically, Anthony Barclay died within one year of his migration to Liberia, but his strong and resourceful widow, Sarah Ann, proved more than capable of the task of raising the Barclay children in a new and difficult environment. Indeed, she was so successful that young Arthur grew up to become President of Liberia in the year 1904!

And it should be noted that Arthur Barclay was no ordinary President: he was highly praised for the great skill that he exhibited in maintaining the independence of Liberia (one of only two independent countries on the continent of Africa) at a time when the European 'scramble for Africa' was at its height. Furthermore, Arthur's nephew Edwin Barclay also attained the Presidency of Liberia in the year 1930.

But not only did the Barbadian community of Liberia produce two presidents—Arthur Barclay and Edwin Barclay—it also produced five secretaries of state, two secretaries of the Treasury, two Attorneys General, and numerous other high officials of state, including judges, senators, Postmasters General, ministers of government and members of Congress. Indeed, Barbadian families such as the Barclays, Bournes, Padmores, Grimes, Wiles, Weekes, Holders and Clarkes became leading elements within Liberian society.

Of course, the negative side of this Barbadian achievement is that the Barbadian immigrants were eventually integrated into the so-called Americo-Liberian elite class of the society, and would therefore have been implicated, to some extent, in the maintenance of an unjust social system that discriminated against the indigenous African citizens of Liberia. However, the fact is that our Barbadian kith and kin are today an integral part of the current population of Liberia.

So now that the nation of Liberia has literally been dismembered before our eyes, and our Liberian brothers and sisters are facing a mind-numbing crisis, what should our response be? I am of the opinion that in light of our historical connections to Liberia, as Barbadians we should be preparing ourselves to make a tangible contribution to the international effort to rebuild Liberia. Granted, we may not have any substantial amounts of capital to contribute, but we can offer the services of technical personnel—nurses, doctors, teachers, administrators, and skilled technicians. We can also offer scholarships in Barbados to some young Liberians in need. We should therefore be seeking to honour the memory of our ancestors who did so much to build a new 'Land of the Free' in Africa by doing our duty to their grandchildren!

Let us, however, get back to the story of Barbados' Pan-Africanist journey. That sterling 19th century Barbadian tradition of Pan-Africanism proceeded to make its way into the 20th century on the back of the Marcus Garvey movement.

Marcus Garvey's **Universal Negro Improvement Association** (UNIA) had an extremely strong base in the Barbados of the 1920s and 30s. Furthermore, Garveyism exerted a significant influence on virtually all of the giants of 20th century Barbadian politics and their organizations. I refer to such personalities as Charles Duncan O'Neale and his nephew, Errol Walton

Barrow. One of the other major political giants of 20th century Barbados—Wynter Crawford—was also deeply connected to Pan-African circles in the USA.

Even the relatively conservative Sir Hugh Springer came out of a Pan-Africanist background as secretary of Dr. Harold Moody's **League of Coloured People** in England. And the fledging Barbados Labour Party got much of its early direction through contacts with Pan-Africanist giant, George Padmore, and through its participation in the historic 5th Pan-African Congress that was held in Manchester, England in 1945.

Another interesting aspect of Barbados' connection to Pan-Africanism was highlighted by the historian Winston James in his outstanding book entitled *Holding Aloft The Banner of Ethiopia* when he reflects on the striking phenomenon of Barbadian migrants producing children who developed into some of the world's most outstanding Pan-Africanists:

> "Many of those celebrated as Trinidadian radicals are also, more often than not, little more than a generation removed from Barbadian soil: Henry Sylvester Williams, the pioneer Pan-Africanist, George Padmore, and C.L.R. James are all of Barbadian ancestry. Seldom noted, too, is the fact that although he was born in St. Croix, Hubert Harrison's mother was of Barbadian origin. Samuel Haynes' father was a Barbadian who served in the old West India Regiment in Africa. On returning to the Caribbean, Samuel Haynes senior moved to Belize, where he settled and fathered thirteen children, including

Samuel (one of the greatest and highest ranked Graveyites). Hubert Crichlow, founder of the British Guiana Labour Union and the father of trade unionism in the British Caribbean, was born in Georgetown, the son of a Barbadian dockworker. Eric Walrond's parents were Barbadian, even though Walrond was himself born in Guyana."

All of this is surely food for thought! But the foregoing—as impressive as it is—does not constitute the full list of the outstanding early 20th century Barbadian Pan-Africanists. Indeed, two of the greatest Barbadian Pan-Africanists of them all are virtually unknown. I refer to Arnold Josiah Ford and his wife, Mignon Inniss Ford.

Arnold Josiah Ford, a Barbadian who hailed from the parish of St. Joseph, was a multi-talented musician and served as the musical director of Marcus Garvey's Universal Negro Improvement Association (UNIA). He composed most of the UNIA's original music, including the Universal Ethiopian Anthem—the unofficial national anthem of the entire black world in the 1920s, 30s, and 40s.

After the Garvey movement went into decline, Arnold and his young Barbadian wife, Mignon, migrated to Ethiopia in the 1930s as leaders of a pioneering group of African-American repatriates. As the aging Arnold struggled to build a new community for his followers, the winds of war began to blow and the Italian fascist dictator, Benito Mussolini, prepared to launch an invasion of Ethiopia. It was in this situation of dire existential crisis that a gravely ill Arnold asked his young wife to make a vow that come what may, she would never abandon Ethiopia. Mignon duly obliged, not only for herself, but for her two infant sons as well.

Soon after, Arnold died, and the dreaded Italian invasion became a reality. Not only did Mignon keep her vow, but she went on to become a partisan in the heroic Ethiopian resistance movement, using her home as a place of refuge for the young resistance fighters and giving them whatever support she could. In fact, several times during the dark years of the Italian occupation she was arrested and taken into custody, but by the grace of God, she survived.

After the war ended and the Italians were expelled from Ethiopia, Mignon, a skilled and resourceful educator, went on to establish a secondary school which became a pioneer in the provision of both co-education and in the development of a modern educational curriculum for the youth of Ethiopia. Indeed, so impressive was "Mrs. Ford's school" that Emperor Haile Selassie personally requested that it be re-christened the 'Princess Zenebe Worq High School' in honour of the Emperor's second daughter who died tragically in 1933. Need-less-to-say, the '**Princess Zenebe Worq High School**' rose to the pinnacle of secondary education in Ethiopia, and Mignon came to be regarded as a national hero of Ethiopia for her work in education.

Other more recent 20th century Barbadian contributions to Pan-Africanism revolve around the agitational and public education role performed by the **Peoples Progressive Movement** (principally Bobby Clarke, Leroy Harewood, Glenroy Straughn) in the 1960s; the anti-apartheid solidarity work of the **Southern Africa Liberation Committee** (Michael Cummins, Claire Kennedy, Viola Davis, Ricky Parris, Norman Faria) in the 1970s; the international Pan-Africanist outreach work of the **Pan-African Movement of Barbados** (Kofi Akobi, Bobby Clarke, David Comissiong, Viola Davis, David Denny) in the 1990s; and the multi-faceted programme of the **Clement Payne Movement** (Martin Cadogan, David Comissiong, David Denny, Onkphra Wells, Thelma Gill-Barnett, Edson Crawford, Bobby Clarke) and its sister organisation the **Israel Lovell Foundation** (Trevor Prescod, Cheryl Hunte, John Howell, Ladepoo Salankey).

Special mention must also be made of the outstanding intellectual work performed by such scholars as Kamau Brathwaite, Sir Hilary Beckles, Trevor Marshall and Dr. Rodney Worrell, as well as of the pioneering role of the state-run **Commission for Pan-African Affairs** which was established in 1998, and which has had three Directors to date: David Comissiong, the late Dr. Ikael Tafari and Dr. Deryck Murray.

Of course, straddling almost all of these developments has been the constant example and activism of the Rastafarian community, as exemplified in the works of such stalwarts as Ikael Tafari, Ras Iral, Ras I-ron and Keturah Babb, as well as the efforts of the Black Muslims like Muhammad Nassar.

I end this short reflection on the Barbadian tradition of Pan-Africanism by reproducing the imperishable lyrics of Arnold Ford's majestic **Universal Ethiopian Anthem**, the most important song in the annals of Pan-Africanism:

"Ethiopia, thou land of our fathers,
Thou land where the gods loved to be,
As storm cloud at night suddenly gathers
Our armies come rushing to thee.
We must in the fight be victorious
When swords are thrust outwards to glean;
For us will the vict'ry be glorious
When led by the red, black and green.

Chorus:
Advance, advance to victory
Let Africa be free;
Advance to meet the foe
Advance to victory,
With the might
Of the red, black and green.

Ethiopia, the tyrant's falling,
Who smote thee upon thy knees
And thy children are lustily calling
From over the distant seas.
Jehovah, the Great One has heard us,
Has noted our sighs and our tears,
With His spirit of Love he has stirred us
To be One through the coming years.

O Jehovah, thou God of the ages
Grant unto our sons that lead
The wisdom Thou gave to Thy sages,

When Israel was sore in need.
Thy voice thro' the dim past has spoken,
Ethiopia shall stretch forth her hand,
By Thee all fetters be broken,
And Heav'n bless our dear mother land"

Chapter 15

MARCUS GARVEY (I)

HAVING examined some great heroes of the 17th, 18th and 19th centuries, let us now take a peek into more contemporary times, and let us begin with Marcus Garvey—arguably the greatest black hero of them all.

Garvey was born in the 19th century, developed to full manhood in the 20th century, and created a philosophy and a programme so farsighted that we shall surely have to wait for the end of the 21st century before we see its total realisation.

Marcus Garvey was born on the Caribbean island of Jamaica on the 17th of August 1887, and the formative years of Garvey's life were lived out in a world full of degradation and harsh oppression for the sons and daughters of Africa. In Garvey's native West Indies, even though slavery had been abolished in 1834, the social structure which had been created during the slavery regime had remained intact, and the order of the day for the black masses was poverty, unemployment, landlessness, institutionalised racism and denial of civil and political rights.

In Africa itself, between 1880 and 1914, the powerful imperialistic nation-states of Europe systematically stole and occupied the territory of Africa, and instituted a colonial regime marked by racial prejudice and segregation. By 1914, the only remaining genuinely independent black African nation was the Kingdom of Ethiopia.

In the United States of America slavery had been brought to an end by President Abraham Lincoln's **Emancipation Proclamation** of 1862 and the American Civil War of 1861-64. Hundreds of thousands of Afro-Americans had fought in the victorious Union Army, and some 68,178 had died in the war. However, after a brief optimistic period of 'reconstruction' in which the freed slaves appeared to be making genuine progress, this development was totally shattered with the introduction of '**Black Segregation Codes**' in the south. Attempts were made in all but name to re-enslave the black masses in the southern United States of America, whereas in the north, the Blacks constituted the most depressed bottom of the urban working class.

It was in this extremely depressing world situation that Marcus Garvey formulated his philosophy of 'black nationalism' and established a movement embracing millions of black people, committed to the unification, redemption and liberation of the African race.

The first plank in Garvey's programme was to instill race pride and self-esteem into black people. Garvey began with the premise that "all beauty, virtue and goodness are the exclusive attributes of no one race...." and proceeded to turn the powerful instruments of education and cultural expression developed by his

Universal Negro Improvement Association (UNIA) to the task of establishing in the minds of his followers that "Black is Beautiful."

Garvey placed great emphasis on the study of black history and the dissemination of information about the African past. He continually stressed that the African had enjoyed a history of which he could be proud and argued that Blacks should begin to recognise their own heroes.

Artistic expression, as far as Garvey was concerned, was to be seen as a powerful tool for liberation.

Garvey himself was a prolific poet of liberation and he insisted that black writers, artists and musicians should use their talents to advance the cause of the race.

Religion was also regarded as an instrument for the furthering of Garvey's programme of race pride. This proud black man found it unacceptable that African people should continue to visualise God in the image of a European. Thus, the 1924 UNIA convention agreed to "the Idealisation of God as a Holy Spirit, without physical form, but a Creature of imaginary semblance of the black race, being of like image and likeness." Another outstanding feature of Garvey's religious programme was the use of a race catechism designed to disabuse the minds of black people of all nations of inferiority, and in particular, of the Hamitic Myth.

Garveyism also put primary emphasis on black self-reliance and economic strength. He recognized that the most important area for black independent effort was the economic area, and that successful political action could only be founded on an independent economic base.

Characteristically, he rejected white philanthropy with the assertion that "We do not want their money; this is a black man's movement." And instead, the UNIA established a large number of independent business enterprises, including laundries, restaurants, groceries, hotels, newspapers and industrial and agricultural schools.

The most potent of Garvey's business enterprises was the **Black Star Line** steamship corporation: steamships owned and operated by thousands of black shareholders. Garvey envisaged that the business enterprises established by UNIA branches and other black entrepreneurs all over the world would be linked into a world-wide system of Pan-African economic cooperation: "Negro producers, Negro distributors, Negro consumers." The Black Star Line was to be the carrier for this trade.

Also central to Garvey's programme was the conviction that black people should be brought into one active community encompassing the whole black world, with an independent 'super-state' in the motherland, Africa, as a base. Garvey therefore set before the eyes of all African people the imperishable goal of African independence.

It is clear to me that Garveyism is still extremely relevant 125 years after the birth of its prime mover!

Chapter 16

MARCUS GARVEY (II)

BARBADOS' first Prime Minister and national hero, Right Excellent Errol Barrow, often used to remark that one of his most profound formative political experiences was being in the Queens Park Steel Shed as a 17-year-old youth and listening to Marcus Garvey address the Barbadian people in October 1937. According to Barrow, the message of black pride, initiative and nationalism that he heard on that occasion stayed with him and helped to shape him into the type of political leader that he became.

But there was nothing unique about Errol Barrow's experience, for virtually every single progressive black 'public man' in Barbados between 1918 and 1940 was influenced and shaped by the Honourable Marcus Garvey and the powerful black nationalist philosophy of Garveyism.

Organized 20th century black Barbadian political and labour activism literally began in 1919 when the Marcus Garvey Movement announced its arrival in Barbados with the establishment of the first of no less than six branches of Garvey's **Universal Negro Improvement Association** (UNIA).

These organisations were led by such outstanding Barbadians as John Beckles, Gladstone Leacock, Israel Lovell, and the female trio of Alexandria Gibbs, Anne Hooper and Dorcas Bennett. And they were the first institutionalised expression of labour and black political activism, at a time when trade unions were still illegal in Barbados and a black run political party was unheard of.

No doubt, one of the reasons for Barbados' ready embrace of Garveyism was that a number of Barbadian migrants in the USA and other parts of the 'Black World' occupied leading roles in the UNIA. For example, the Barbadian Arnold Josiah Forde was the Musical Director of the UNIA and composed most of the Movement's stirring anthems and hymns, including the *Universal Ethiopian Anthem*, the unofficial national anthem of the entire Black World in the 1920s and 30s.

And so, the UNIA was the essential foundation on which virtually all of the subsequent Barbadian political and labour organisations were built, including the **Democratic League**, the **Workingmen's Association**, the **Barbados Labour Party**, the **Barbados Workers' Union**, and the **Congress Party**. A roll call of Barbadian activists who were either members of the UNIA or were significantly influenced by Marcus Garvey would include Charles Duncan O'Neal, Clennel Wickham, James A. Tudor, Clement Payne, Menzies Chase, Chrissie Brathwaite, J. A. Martineau, Moses Small, J.T.C. Ramsay, Rawle Parkinson, Dr. Hugh Gordon Cummins, Ulric Grant, Herbert Seale, Sir Hugh Springer and Wynter Crawford, among many others. This list of names alone should indicate that the Barbadian society that we inhabit today would not have emerged without the seminal influence of Marcus Garvey!

In light of this history and record it makes eminent sense for the Barbadian people to see in Marcus Garvey a man who made such a tremendous contribution to the development of Barbados that he deserves to be honoured and memorialized in our country. Can you imagine that we have a George Washington House and a Queen Elizabeth Hospital in Barbados, but no edifice or institution named in honour of the great Marcus Garvey?

It is against this background therefore that I have no difficulty whatsoever in supporting the proposal of the **Clement Payne Movement** of Barbados that the Queens Park Steel Shed be re-named the **Marcus Garvey Steel Shed**, since Marcus Garvey and the philosophy of Garveyism are woven into the very spirit, culture and ethos of Barbados.

Chapter 17

THE WORLD'S GREATEST GARVEYITE

ONE cannot mention the name Marcus Garvey in a Barbadian context without attaching it to the name Martin Cadogan—a great son of Barbados and one of the most committed followers of Marcus Garvey.

I would now like to pay tribute to this unforgettable Barbadian and Caribbean Pan-Africanist who recently departed this earthly scene and has gone on to the ancestral realm.

I now do so by reproducing the tribute that I penned to my comrade and mentor, Martin 'Rudy' Cadogan, at the time of his tragic death:

"Barbados should be in mourning today!

Our national flag should be flying at half mast, solemn music should be playing on the radio, and the people of Barbados should be preparing themselves to say a final farewell to one of our outstanding sons of the soil. I speak of none other than the great black nationalist 'warrior' and patriot, Martin Cadogan.

It is hard for us to accept it but it is true; Martin Cadogan is dead. He slipped away from us at the Queen Elizabeth Hospital on the evening of Thursday 8th July 2004.

Anyone who ever met Martin Cadogan, or heard him speaking, immediately knew that they were in the presence of a unique and profoundly committed human being.

Martin was perhaps the world's greatest devotee of the Honourable Marcus Garvey: there was a palpable spiritual link between Martin and the great Jamaican father of African Nationalism who died in the City of London when Martin was a toddler growing up in the rural parish of St. Peter in Barbados.

Martin devoted his life to defending the name of Marcus Garvey, and spreading the good news of the programme and ideology of Garvey's **Universal Negro Improvement Association**. As far as Martin was concerned the only book that was required reading for every single black man and woman was *The Philosophy And Opinions of Marcus Garvey*! And if today in Barbados there is some general appreciation of the work and ideas of Marcus Garvey, a tremendous amount of the credit must be given to Martin Cadogan.

Brother Cadogan was also perhaps Barbados' last living link to the epoch making Black nationalist movement of 1960s America. After having excelled in Barbados as a police officer and athlete, Martin migrated to the city of New York in the 1960s where he found his true calling— **Black Nationalism**.

In the USA, Martin rubbed shoulders with some of the greatest fighters for black dignity and power: Stokely Carmichael, Muhammad Ali, and most importantly, Carlos Cooks and the officers and members of the

African Nationalist Pioneer Movement.

The legendary Carlos Cooks was the critical 'underground' black revolutionary who, in the 1940s and 50s, played a key role in keeping the ideas of Garveyism alive in the USA, and passing them on to new and young activists such as Malcolm X.

As a member of Cook's **African Nationalist Pioneer Movement**, Martin Cadogan, known in North America by the assumed name of 'Rudy', was involved in some of the most important 'on-the-ground' and 'underground' agitational work that drove forward the national **Civil Rights Movement** of the USA.

Martin played an important role in the successful campaign to have Black Studies programmes established at American universities. He himself graduated from university in New York with a degree in accounting, secured a job on Wall Street, and immediately rocked that elitist centre of world capitalism when he took to setting up his microphone and speakers on Wall Street in order to preach **Black Nationalism** and revolution.

As the 1960s came to an end, and the brutal repression and assassination of Black Panther and African Nationalist activists gathered pace in the USA, Rudy escaped to Canada where he continued to struggle on behalf of his beloved Black people.

Brother Cadogan ultimately returned to Barbados in the late 1970s and consciously took upon himself the mission of sowing the seeds of Garveyism and Cook's 'African Nationalist Pioneer' philosophy in Barbados.

He was one of the key members of the **Clement**

Payne Movement, and played a critical role in securing the elevation of Clement Payne and Bussa as national heroes, and the designation of **Emancipation Day** as a public holiday in Barbados.

Martin defended the cause of the imprisoned Nelson Mandela, assisted and befriended numerous ANC activists and ran three elections against Prime Minister Owen Arthur on a platform of "Free Nelson Mandela", "return to Local Government", and "develop a third political party." At the time many Barbadians could not understand where Martin was coming from, but as the years rolled on and Mandela was released, the **National Democratic Party** of Barbados was formed, and many voices clamoured for a de-centralisation of government, Martin's extra-ordinary vision was better appreciated.

Martin was an influential member of the National Democratic Party and played an important role in bringing down the backward and destructive **Democratic Labour Party** Administration of Prime Minister Erskine Sandiford in 1994.

He was a friend and critical mentor of a whole generation of younger nationalists and Pan-Africanists in Barbados."

Chapter 18

LAMMING, SOBERS & RIHANNA

GEORGE Lamming, Sir Garfield Sobers and Rihanna—three outstanding citizens of the little 166 square mile Caribbean island of Barbados. One wonders if we Barbadian people truly understand the significance of these three national icons, and the profound message that is wrapped up in their lives and careers.

Let us begin with Lamming. In the year 1950, George Lamming traveled from the Caribbean to England and immediately proceeded to write *In The Castle Of My Skin*, a novel that demonstrated such a mastery of the English language and contained such compelling philosophical and poetic insights that it catapulted him to the top of that most remarkable phenomenon of world literature, the newly emergent school of West Indian novelists. Lamming was a mere 23 years of age.

In 1958, Garfield Sobers, the Barbadian and West Indies all-round cricketer, batted for 10 hours against the Pakistani test team at Sabina Park in Jamaica and broke the world test cricket batting record with a scintillating 365 not out that confirmed his total mastery of the game of Cricket. Sobers was 21 years old.

And in the two year period of 2006 to 2007,

Rihanna dominated the international music charts, demonstrating a profound understanding of the nuances of contemporary rhythm & blues music and copping numerous international awards along the way, including Billboard's 'Pop Artiste Of The Year'. Amazingly, her product sales outshone anything that such legends as Michael Jackson and Elvis Presley had been able to achieve in the similar beginning phases of their remarkable careers. Rihanna's phenomenal breakthrough came at the tender age of 17 years.

What is particularly remarkable about these achievements is the 'precociousness' of it all. By any measure, the accomplishments of Lamming, Sobers and Rihanna bear the marks of genius, but to achieve these remarkable feats at such young ages places them in a most elevated category.

It should be noted that they each had to master either a language, an art form or a sporting discipline that had its roots in a nation very different from ours, and that had been created by people other than ourselves. In spite of this, they were still able to use the insights and techniques that they had worked out for themselves to express our own unique Barbadian and Caribbean instincts within the medium, thereby adding something new to the medium.

But what I really wish to draw special attention to is that these three outstanding individuals were born, bred and nurtured in the unique geographical, historical and socio-economic environment of little Barbados!

The unique genius of George Lamming was forged in

the wake of the 1937 riots that shook up the restrictive racist Barbadian society and was centred around the working-class district of Carrington Village and the lower middle class based Combermere School, while Sobers emerged from the small village of the Bay Land, the workers' Barbados Cricket League (BCL), and the social and nationalist sentiments that came to the fore in the Barbados of the 1950's. Rihanna, for her part, is a product of a very familiar Barbadian upbringing centered around the City district of Westbury Road, and such quintessential Barbadian schools as Charles F. Broome Primary and Combermere.

Yet, in spite of the seeming parochialism and narrow Bajan-ness of their upbringing and socialization, these three 'international precedent-setters' were able to master the international mediums in which they chose to express themselves—the English Language, the game of Cricket and the genre of contemporary rhythm & blues music—and to add to that technical mastery uniquely Barbadian and Caribbean insights, essences and instincts that arise out of our local environment.

I therefore wish to adopt the reasoning and insights of the great Caribbean philosopher, Cyril Lionel Robert James, and to make, on behalf of my Barbadian island home, the expansive claim that our history and geography have conspired to create a society that is capable of producing the most outstanding accomplishments in virtually all spheres of human endeavour.

The eminent C.L.R. James was fond of comparing not only Barbados, but all of our Caribbean societies, to the 'city states' of ancient Greece—the city states that produced such giants as Socrates, Plato, Solon, Pythagoras, Pericles and Archimedes. James discerned in our small size and in the intimacy of our social and political culture, a recipe for creativity and rapid cultural advancement that is comparable with what obtained in Greece in its most creative classical period.

James maintained that Barbados and the other Caribbean island-states are pregnant with the potential for the establishment of a truly authentic form of democracy. He looked at the geography of our island-homes and discerned that "democracy presses on us from the very physical environment in which we live."

For him, democracy, or creative people power and self-expression, is bound up with the small size of our societies. Our states, like the Greek city states, are so small that everybody has a grasp of what is going on, and virtually nobody is 'backward', in the sense of being remote and far removed from the sphere of national public activity. It is in this type of environment that citizens can create and engage in a powerful and conscious type of 'speech'—'living speech' that has the power to unite the people and to create civic energy, enthusiasm and passion.

Furthermore, James noted that not only are we Caribbean people the masters of very highly developed modern languages, but that we also have at our disposal highly advanced instruments of communication in the form of radio, television, airlines and film. And of course, in the current era, we would have to add the internet.

All of these factors combine to produce uniquely creative societies that, once they are prepared to look inward and to boldly confront and overcome their internal differences and contradictions, are able to move far and fast, to leap from social position to social position, to make cultural and intellectual discoveries and inventions, and to nurture and produce outstanding world historical personalities.

I therefore wish to concur with C.L.R. James. With Lamming, Sobers and Rihanna we have but an inkling of the enormous potential of one little Caribbean society. I urge the masses of our people to recognise that Caribbean people are capable of a greatness that will astound the world. Let us therefore resolve to throw off all the 'dead-weight' that is currently holding us back and get on with it!

Chapter 19

THE QUIET WARRIOR

ONE of the striking features of Barbados' famous public monument known variously as the Bussa Statue and as the Emancipation Statue is the following very powerful and moving inscription at the base of the monument:

> Let my children
> rise
> in the path
> of the morning
> up and go forth
> on the road
> of the morning
> run through the fields
> in the sun
> of the morning,
> see the rainbow
> of Heaven:
> God's curved
> mourning
> calling.

This powerful piece of verse is the creation of Barbados' most outstanding poet, historian and Culture scholar—Kamau Brathwaite—and is taken from the poem entitled "Tom" and published in Brathwaite's universally acclaimed poetry collection known as *The Arrivants*.

It is entirely fitting that Kamau Brathwaite's work should be inscribed on the one piece of Barbadian public art that is dedicated to the quest of the African-Barbadian for liberation, for Kamau Brathwaite is perhaps the most outstanding example of a Barbadian who has transcended the spiritual and psychological limitations and constraints of Barbados' colonial heritage.

In Kamau Brathwaite, Barbadians possess the living example of an extremely creative and intellectually gifted son of the soil who has taken it upon himself to make that necessary inward journey towards the core of his being as a child of Africa transplanted in the New World and shaped by the powerful dialectical (or 'tidelectical') cultural currents of '**Plantation America**'.

And because of the magnitude and integrity of Kamau's effort, Barbados has received the inestimable gift of a profound native philosopher and creative artist whose work has helped to clarify many of the critical cultural and other existential challenges that we face as a nation.

But who exactly is this Kamau Brathwaite—this quiet warrior—who lives among us at his modest Cow Pasture, Christ Church home, and whose shepherd-like spirit still watches over our nation? Let us spend some time looking more closely at the intimate details of the life of this great Barbadian.

Kamau was born in Barbados in the year 1930 into what was known in those days as a 'coloured middle-class oriented family', and was actually christened

'Edward Brathwaite' by his parents, Edward and Beryl Brathwaite. (The African name of Kamau—which means 'Quiet Warrior'—was bestowed upon him much later in life by the famous Kenyan writer, Ngugi wa Thiong'o and other African soul-mates during a sojourn in Kenya.)

As a child, young Edward Brathwaite grew up between Mile and a Quarter in St. Peter and Bay Street (Brown's Beach) in St. Michael, and attended such well known primary schools as St. Matthias, St. Mary's and Bay Street Primary.

His secondary schooling began at Combermere, where he spent two years before his parents secured a transfer to Harrison College. And this is how Kamau has described his stint at Harrison College:

"I went to a secondary school originally founded for children of the plantocracy, colonial civil servants and white professionals; but by the time I got there, the social revolution of the 30's was in full swing, and I was able to make friends with boys of stubbornly non-middle class origin.

I was fortunate, also, with my teachers... they were (with two or three exceptions) happily inefficient as teachers, and none of them seemed to have a stake or interest in our society. We were literally left alone. We picked up what we could or what we wanted from each other and from the few books prescribed like Holy Scripture. With the help of my parents, I applied to do Modern Studies (History and English) in the sixth form... and succeeded, to everyone's surprise, in winning one of the Island Scholarships that traditionally took the ex-planters' sons 'home' to Oxbridge or London."

So these are the bare facts of Kamau's upbringing in colonial-era Barbados. Some twenty years later, Kamau explained the deeper significance of this upbringing in a very important essay entitled Timheri:

"...my education and background, though nominally 'middle class', is, on examination, not of this nature at all. I had spent most of my boyhood on the beach and in the sea with 'beach-boys', or in the country, at my grandfather's with country boys and girls. I was therefore not in a position to make any serious intellectual investment in West Indian middle class values. But since I was not then consciously aware of any other West Indian alternative (though in fact I had been living that alternative), I found and felt myself 'rootless' on arrival in England, and like so many other West Indians of the time, more than ready to accept and absorb the culture of the Mother Country. I was, in other words, a potential Afro-Saxon."

But fortunately for Kamau (and for our society), two things saved this great son of the soil from degeneration into a colonial-minded 'Afro-Saxon'. One was the appearance, in 1953, of George Lamming's seminal Barbadian novel *In The Castle of My Skin*, with its exploration of the unique nuances of the culture, sociology and landscapes of Barbados, and its vindication of our Barbadianism and West Indianism.

The other was that upon graduating from Cambridge University in 1955 with a degree in History, the young historian and educator secured a job as an Education Officer in the West African colony of the Gold Coast (now the independent nation of Ghana). For Kamau this was very much a type of spiritual homecoming—a notion that he expressed in his poem entitled "The New Ships" as follows:

Takoradi was hot.
Green struggled through red
as we landed.

Laterite lanes drifted off
into dust
into silence.

Mammies crowded with cloths,
flowered and laughed;
white teeth
smooth voices like pebbles
moved by the sea of their language.

Akwaaba they smiled
meaning welcome

akwaaba they called
aye kooo

well have you walked
have you journeyed

welcome
you who have come

> back a stranger
> after three hundred years
>
> welcome

Kamau spent eight years in Ghana, during which time he not only got to know the country and its people intimately through his work as an educator, but with the help of his Guyana born wife—Doris Welcome aka Zea Mexican—he also developed a Children's Theatre which produced several of the African-themed plays that he authored in Ghana.

This was a time of important inward spiritual growth for the Barbadian historian/educator/playwright/poet, an experience that he explained in "Timheri" as follows:

"Slowly, slowly, ever so slowly; obscurely, slowly but surely, during the eight years I lived there, I was coming to an awareness and understanding of community, of cultural wholeness, of the place of the individual within the tribe, in society. Slowly, slowly, ever so slowly, I came to a sense of identification of myself with these people, my living diviners. I came to connect my history with theirs, the bridge of my mind now linking Atlantic and ancestor, homeland and heartland."

Simply put, Kamau had discovered his intrinsic 'African-ness', not an African-ness that made him identical with the new brothers and sisters that he discovered in Ghana, but rather, an African-ness that had been shaped by the dislocation of the Middle Passage and the centuries of experiences in Plantation America.

But perhaps I should let Kamau speak for himself:

"When I turned to leave, I was no longer a lonely individual talent: there was something wider, more subtle—the self without ego—without arrogance. And I came home to find that I had not really left. That it was still Africa. Africa in the Caribbean. The middle passage had now guessed its end. The connection between my lived, but unheeded non-middle class boyhood, and its Great Tradition on the eastern (African) mainland had been made."

In 1962 Brathwaite came home not only to a University of the West Indies teaching job, but also to find himself face to face with the West Indian Independence Movement that saw Jamaica and Trinidad and Tobago securing their independence in 1962, to be followed by Guyana and Barbados in 1966.

It was in this milieu, and with this new understanding of himself, that Kamau Brathwaite produced some of the most outstanding poetry of the 20th and 21st centuries! A partial listing of his most important volumes of poetry is as follows:

Rights of Passage (1967);

Masks (1968);

Islands (1969);

The Arrivants (1973);

Mother Poem (1977);

Sun Poem (1982);

X-Self (1987);

The Zea Mexican Diary (1993);

Dream Stories (1994);

Barabajan Poems (1994);
Trench Town Rock (1999);
Ancestors (2001);
Magical Realism (2002); and
Born To Slow Horses (2005).

What distinguishes Kamu Brathwaite's body of work is that he consciously sought to use and valorise quintessential aspects of our Barbadian/Caribbean/Afro-American/Pan-African culture. Thus, the rhythmic structure of his poetry ranges from Jazz to Calypso, Limbo, Rasta drumming, and to the rhythms and intonations of the Spiritual Baptists and the practitioners of the West African derived Orisha and Vodun religions.

Kamau also used his poetry as a vehicle to search for our 'Nam' or inner essence as a people—an exploration that caused him to lift up and explore our 'Nation Language' (commonly condescendingly referred to as 'dialect'), and to pierce beneath the surface of our Caribbean landscapes and culturescapes to discern ancestors, African orishas, and fecund and original creation myths and cultural insights.

This body of work is far too voluminous and profound to deal with in greater detail within the confines of this short essay, but there is one special poem that I would to focus on and bring forcefully to my readers' attention. To my mind, this poem is the quintessential poem of the Caribbean independence era! It is entitled 'Negus' and was first published way back in 1969, in the early years of Independence. It was relevant then, and it is perhaps even more relevant today. It is a poem that every single Caribbean citizen should know by heart.

Let us therefore conclude this essay with an excerpt from Negus:

It
it
it
it is not

it is not
it is not
it is not enough
it is not enough to be free
of the red white and blue
of the drag, of the dragon

it is not
it is not
it is not enough
it is not enough to be free
of the whips, principalities and powers
where is your kingdom of the Word?

it is not
it is not
it is not enough
it is not enough to be free
of malarial fevers, fear of the hurricane,
fear of invasions, crops' drought, fire's
blisters upon the cane

It is not
it is not
it is not enough

to be able to fly to Miami,
structure skyscrapers, excavate the moon
scaped seashore sands to build hotels, casinos,
sepulchres

It is not
it is not
it is not enough
it is not enough to be free
to bulldoze god's squatters from their tunes,
from their relics
from their tombs of drums

It is not enough
to pray to Barclays bankers on the telephone
to Jesus Christ by short wave radio
to the United States marines by rattling your hip
bones

I
must be given words to shape my name
to the syllables of trees

I
must be given words to refashion futures
like a healer's hand

I
must be given words so that the bees
in my blood's buzzing brain of memory

will make flowers, will make flocks of birds,
will make sky, will make heaven,
the heaven open to the thunder-stone and the
volcano and the un-folding land

It is not
it is not
it is not enough
to be pause, to be hole
to be void, to be silent
to be semicolon, to be semicolony;

Chapter 20

WE ARE A CARIBBEAN CIVILIZATION

UP to this stage we have focused quite a lot on ourselves as Barbadians, as citizens of this small 166 sq. mile island-nation known as Barbados. But there can be no doubt that our Barbados is but one parish in the wider 'nation' known as 'the Caribbean'. It is therefore time that we look a little more closely at our Caribbean-ness.

At the 1986 CARICOM heads of government conference, the late Errol Barrow made a most insightful observation about the Barbadian and Caribbean people:

> "If we have sometimes failed to comprehend the essence of the regional integration movement, the truth is that thousands of ordinary Caribbean people do, in fact, live that reality every day. In Barbados, our families are no longer exclusively Barbadian by island origin. We have Barbadian children of Jamaican mothers; Barbadian children of Antiguan and St. Lucian fathers... We are a family of islands..."

Mr. Barrow knew exactly what he was talking about; after all, his own father, Bishop Reginald Barrow, had been born in St. Vincent, his uncle Dr. Charles Duncan

O'Neale had Tobagonian antecedents and had lived and worked in Dominica and Trinidad, and Mr. Barrow himself had been partially educated in the Virgin Islands.

My own experience is not unlike that of Mr. Barrow. My mother is Barbadian but grew up in Guyana, my father was a Grenadian who lived and worked in eight different Caribbean territories, and my three brothers were born in Trinidad, Guyana and St. Vincent.

The point that Mr. Barrow went on to make, after drawing attention to the inter-connected island nationalities within Caribbean families, was that all Caribbean people are part of and share in a common 'storehouse' of historical traditions, knowledge, wisdom, and artistic, social, political and economic inventions. In other words, the people who inhabit these Caribbean territories, from Cuba in the north to Guyana in the south, have, over the centuries, created a common and unique culture—a Caribbean civilization.

One of my strongest impressions of Errol Barrow was that he was one of the few Caribbean leaders who were aware of the immense variety, uniqueness and value of our Caribbean civilization. I also suspected that this awareness constituted a large part of the foundation upon which his sense of dignity and self-confidence was built.

There can be no doubt that we are indeed the possessors of a valuable civilisation which has the potential to develop into a beacon of creativity and humanism to the rest of the world. A brief overview of our Caribbean experience will suffice to substantiate the point.

The Caribbean people have been the creators of unique social inventions in the spheres of religion, politics, art, sport and economic organization.

Our religious heritage ranges from Cuban Santeria through Trinidadian Shango, Haitian Vodun, Jamaican Pocomania and Rastafarianism, to the numerous Afro-Baptist and Afro-Protestant churches so prevalent in Barbados.

In politics and economics, our heritage includes our role in fuelling and sustaining the **Industrial Revolution** of Europe, Toussaint L'Ouverture and the **Haitian Revolution**, Marcus Garvey and George Padmore, **Black Nationalism** and **Pan-Africanism**, the **Cuban Revolution**, Stokely Carmichael and **Black Power**. And our experiments in political structure run the gamut from Cuban socialism to Third World liberal parliamentary democracy.

In music, we have created the steel drum, the Cuban conga, calypso, reggae, spouge, salsa, meringue, cadence, zouk and numerous varieties of folk music. Our dance spawned the calenda, the National Ballet of Cuba and a variety of Jamaican, Trinidadian and French and Dutch Antillean dance traditions.

A military tradition has been marked out by Cudjoe the maroon, Antonio Maceo and Toussaint, while geniuses like Sir Garfield Sobers, Sir Vivian Richards, Teofilo Stevenson, Sammy Soso, Usain Bolt and Merlene Ottey have created a distinct sporting tradition and style.

Our intellectual successes include Aime Cesaire and Negritude, Jose Marti, Jean Price-Mars, Frantz Fanon,

Alexandre Dumas, C.L.R. James and the school of English-speaking Caribbean writers, including George Lamming and Edward Kamau Brathwaite. And over the last 40 years, a contemporary intellectual tradition rooted in the realities of Caribbean life and centred around the University of the West Indies has developed. A substantial body of development-based intellectual work has been created, utilizing all of the tools of modern scientific analysis, including the Marxist system of theorizing.

These latter day intellects include economists like Clive Thomas, Arthur Lewis, Norman Girvan and George Beckford; historians like Elsa Goveia, Walter Rodney, Douglas Hall, Hilary Beckles and Gordon Lewis; and political scientists such as Carl Stone and Lloyd Best.

Surely the task of any serious leader, politician or political party in the Caribbean today must be to bring home to our people their stake in our Caribbean civilization, and to utilize the enormous store of Caribbean collective wisdom and intellectual work to enlighten the path that lies ahead of us as a people.

We are one region, and if we are to have an acceptable future as an independent, progressive people with an identity of our own, then we must begin to think and act as a Caribbean family, making full use of our native intellect, ingenuity and natural resources.

Chapter 21

BARBADOS IS THE FATHER OF CARIBBEAN INTEGRATION

THE EUROPEANS who enslaved our African forefathers, who forcibly transported them across the Atlantic ocean, and who split them up by depositing them on a number of small Caribbean islands, intended—by that process—to make the black population of the Caribbean into a permanently weak and divided people.

It is important that the black people of Barbados and other Caribbean nations recognise that when the slave ships stopped at the various Caribbean harbours that the white enslavers often separated African family members from each other and deposited them in different island colonies.

But don't simply take it from me. Read instead the words of Olaudah Equiano, the famous African who was enslaved in the 1700s, and who, having been transported across the 'middle passage' to Barbados, was subjected to the horrors of the Bridgetown slave market before the slave ship moved on to another port:

> "...the buyers rush at once into the yard where the slaves are confined... without scruple, are relations and friends separated, most of them

never to see each other again... there were several brothers, who, in the sale, were sold in different lots; and it was very moving on this occasion to see and hear their cries at parting... Why are parents to lose their children, brothers their sisters, or husbands their wives?"

So the point is that from as far back as the early stages of colonisation and enslavement there has been a reality of black 'kith and kin' being divided up and separated from each other, and living in a multiplicity of small European colonies known as Barbados, St. Kitts, Jamaica, St. Lucia, St. Vincent, Grenada and the list goes on.

Furthermore, whenever any serious efforts were made by the black people of the Caribbean to counteract this European-orchestrated agenda of separatism and weakness and to attempt to unite themselves as a people across these artificially created small-island nations, our historical oppressors have done everything possible to subvert and suppress such efforts.

But again, don't simply take it from me. Rather, let us examine the case of our national hero, Rt. Excellent Samuel Jackman Prescod, and his mid-19th century effort to unite the black and so-called 'coloured' people of the English-speaking Caribbean islands.

The laying of the foundations of the regional integration movement was actually a Barbadian enterprise that was launched in the mid 19th century by Samuel Jackman Prescod through the establishment of his organisation known as the 'Colonial Union of Coloured People' (CUCP). This was a pioneering Caribbean organisation that, in the words of Prescod's biographer, Dr. Alana Johnson, was dedicated to creating "a black West Indian federation by eliminating the separation and insularity which divided communities across the colonies... Its first objective was to provide full equality for all Afro-Caribbean people."

And how did the white Barbadians of Prescod's day respond to this pioneering effort of regional integration, black unity and self-empowerment? Well, Dr. Alana Johnson informs us as follows:

> "Whites who wished to maintain white supremacy as the blueprint for post slavery society were horrified, because they feared its scope and magnitude. For them, it was tantamount to an act of war... They launched a counter-attack and decided to use the island's parliament to rid Barbados of the union."

Alana Johnson also goes on to tell us that "Prescod was not deterred... he travelled to other islands to launch the plan within the context of planter hysteria... he was warmly received and supported by blacks and some coloureds, particularly those who subscribed to his race dignity doctrine".

And so, Samuel Jackman Prescod was the quintessential role model for other outstanding Barbadian architects of the regional integration movement such as Hubert Crichlow (son of a Barbadian and founder of the British West Indies and Guyana Labour Congress); Sir Grantley Adams (Premier of the West Indies Federation);

Richard B. Moore and Reginald Pierrepoint (New York based champions of West Indian Federation); Wynter Crawford and Erskine Ward (Champions of an Eastern Caribbean Federation); Rt. Excellent Errol Barrow (chief architect of CARIFTA and CARICOM); Fred Cozier (first Secretary General of CARICOM); Kurleigh King (Secretary General of CARICOM); Sir Neville Nicholls (President of the Caribbean Development Bank); and Owen Arthur (chief architect of the CSME).

The point is that Barbados has always been in the forefront of the regional integration movement. Thus, if there is any single CARICOM country that can legitimately claim ownership of the '**Treaty of Chaguaramas**' and of the integration process that it set in motion, that country is surely Barbados.

But again, don't simply take it from me. Let us instead refer to the explanation that Rt. Excellent Errol Barrow gave of the genesis of both CARIFTA and CARICOM during his address at the signing ceremony of the Treaty of Chaguaramas on 4th July 1973:

> "I can now disclose that it was on the 4th July, 1965, that the Prime Minister of Guyana met with me in Barbados, at my invitation, to discuss the possibility of establishing a free trade area between our two countries in the first instance, and the rest of the Caribbean at such time as they would be ready to follow our example... I invited the Prime Minister of Guyana to come to Barbados so that we could hold these discussions and today, I am very happy to be here, some eight years later to be a signatory... So Mr. Chairman,

it was on the 4th July 1965 one small step for two
countries. Today as a signatory to this agreement
... it is a giant step for all of us."

It is against this background therefore that we denounce
and repudiate all of those self-serving opportunists who
have pounced upon the recent Shanique Myrie decision
of the Caribbean Court of Justice, and have sought to use
it to attack the very concept of Caribbean integration and
to suggest that the Treaty of Chaguaramas is something
that is foreign and hostile to Barbados and Barbadians.

We are not fools. We know the history, and we therefore
know exactly where they are coming from and what
they wish to achieve. Like Samuel Jackman Prescod, like
Errol Barrow, and like all the other Barbadian architects
of Caribbean integration and black self-empowerment,
we will not be deterred, and will march onwards to our
ultimate destiny of a powerful, unified Caribbean nation
and civilization.

Chapter 22

HISTORIC MISTAKE THAT MUST BE CORRECTED

IF we are to ever achieve the goal of a powerful, unified Caribbean nation and civilization, there are some historic developmental mistakes that we have made and that we must correct as a matter of urgency.

Barbados, like virtually every other black nation on the face of this earth, suffers from the major deficiency of a lack of industrial production capacity, as well as from a lack of high technology capacity in other spheres of economic activity.

And over the past five years of international recession, the pernicious effects of this deficiency have become only too obvious, as Barbados has assumed the appearance of an impotent nation, with its leaders reduced to woefully and helplessly waiting and hoping that the North Atlantic countries would come to their rescue with a resuscitation of the flow of white tourists from the USA, Britain and Canada.

The sad thing is that it did not have to be this way. Back in 1966, when Barbados embarked upon its journey of Independence, the then leaders of our country, faced with having to decide upon a major strategy of economic development, made the wrong choice of opting for a path of tourism-based development.

Barbados' approach may be contrasted with that of Singapore, a similar small island developing nation with little or no natural resources that became independent in 1965. Faced with a similar choice, the political leader of Singapore, Prime Minister Lee Kwan Yew—a lawyer who had been a contemporary of Errol Barrow at the London School of Economics—opted for the opposite path of industrialisation.

Prime Minister Yew has acknowledged in his memoirs that, faced with the daunting problem of endemic unemployment, the newly independent Singapore did turn to tourism for the first two years of its Independence journey, since tourism required little capital. But he quickly goes on to point out that he and his cabinet colleagues were clear that tourism could only be a temporary stop-gap measure, and that the long term survival and development of Singapore would hinge upon industrial development and the establishment of factories in Singapore.

Furthermore, the leaders of Singapore not only opted for industrialisation, but consciously set out to give their country a technological capacity that would permit it to provide indispensable functions for industrial companies engaged in the most advanced, high technology production. And, of course, once Singapore had developed that aptitude in relation to manufacturing industry, it was able to carry it over into areas of sophisticated, high priced services such as banking, shipping, medical services, education and financial services.

If we fast forward some 48 years to 2013, we can see how right Lee Kwan Yew was. Today, Singapore is one of the most successful nations in the world, with a powerful economy based on electronics, chemical engineering, mechanical engineering, machine production, biomedical services, financial services, petroleum refining, shipping and ship repairs, and with a per capita Gross Domestic Product of US $60,688.00—the third highest in the world.

I wish to stress that the leader of Singapore had been guided by the notion that the people of Singapore must be given the capacity to play a critical role in disseminating the benefits created by the forms of industrial production that are based on the newest and most sophisticated advances in technology. As a result, Singapore has not only developed the capacity for the high technology of the past half-century, but has also consciously positioned itself to be in the thick of things as it anticipates futuristic high technology developments in computer technology, micro-biology, gene therapy, cloning, organ reproduction and other cutting edge areas of knowledge.

How do we in Barbados compare? Well, the sad truth is that we have been left way behind, and are still at the level of agitating ourselves over how we can better serve and please the European and North American tourists that we are able to attract to our shores to enjoy our sea, sand and sun.

The trouble with us is that we have set our sights too low, and have been satisfied with too little. Clearly, we are not a people who are bereft of intelligence and ability. Indeed, we recently received a very pleasant reminder of the outstanding intellectual potential of our people when the story of Allan Emptage, the Barbadian computer scientist who invented the Internet search engine, hit the international news headlines. It brought home to us that it was a Barbadian who gave the world the critical invention that has permitted Google, Yahoo, Altavista and all the others to establish their multi-billion dollar enterprises.

The question we should therefore be asking ourselves is: how many other potential Allan Emptages are there among the tens of thousands of students that are being educated in our Barbadian schools?

There is no reason why we cannot set out to replicate the Singapore example by taking our people to a level where they become indispensable collaborators in the world's most advanced and sophisticated systems of production.

And, if we adopted such an ambition and approach, we too need not restrict it only to the sphere of manufacturing or industrial production. Rather, we could also extend it to putting Barbados in the forefront of new, cutting edge developments in the Arts, the Humanities, in Education, and in the provision of a range of sophisticated, high priced professional services as well.

Of course, if any of this is to be accomplished, it will require a revolution in Education in Barbados. It will also require that a new way of thinking take hold at the highest levels of government. Too ambitious and idealistic you say! Well, I don't think so. I don't think that anything is beyond the capacity of the Barbadian people!

Chapter 23

THE EMPEROR IS NAKED

BUT whatever weaknesses and deficiencies we possess, let us not lose sight of the fact that we do possess strengths as well; and sometimes, when we assess ourselves against the backdrop of the actions and behaviour of some of the largest and most powerful nations of the world, we recognize that we bring (and can continue to bring) something of inestimable value to world civilisation. Let us reflect on just one example of this.

Back in the month of May 2011 the political and economic leaders of the United States of America (USA) and their multi-national media corporations proclaimed to the world that the USA's assassination of Osama bin Laden was an act of national greatness.

Well, we should all just pause for a while and soberly consider precisely what message this proclamation imparted to impressionable children and adolescents all over the world.

Our children were told that it is the ultimate in greatness for a large and powerful nation to send a team of its most ferocious military warriors to invade the territory of another much weaker country; to corner an unarmed physically decrepit old man; and, in the absence of this man ever having been subjected to any judicial process of trial and conviction, to cold-bloodedly shoot him to death in the presence of his wife and children. This, the youth of the world were assured, is not just national greatness, but the ultimate in national greatness!

Somebody—some small and morally clear-sighted nation—has to tell the 'Emperor' that he is naked, and that his actions are a perversion and a repudiation of international law, and of the sacred principles of justice and morality. And so, acting on behalf of and in the name of the people of Barbados, we say: let little Barbados accept this challenge of speaking truth to the powerful, pompasetting, morally deluded USA.

You see, the citizen of Barbados is the citizen of a country whose government has never invaded any other country; never bombed any foreign city; never carried out any political assassination; nor ever committed any other crime against humanity.

Many of us in Barbados often wonder what it must feel like to be the citizen of a country whose government routinely murders and exterminates other human beings in one's name. What, we wonder, does it feel like to be the citizen of a nation that exterminated three million Vietnamese; that dropped two atomic bombs on Hiroshima and Nagasaki; that wiped out hundreds of thousands of Iraqis; that has carried out scores of illegal foreign invasions; and that has assassinated foreign leaders ranging from Africa's Patrice Lumumba to Latin America's Salvador Allende? How is the average

American citizen able to live with the consciousness that such acts of barbarity are routinely committed in his or her name?

But in addition to this, little Barbados is also qualified to point out the Emperor's nakedness for another reason; long before September 11, 2001, we experienced our own version of 911.

We would like to remind the world that on the 6th of October 1976—almost exactly 25 years before September 11, 2001—the 250,000 people of Barbados had to deal with the horrific tragedy of having a Cuban civilian airliner, filled to capacity with 73 passengers, blown out of our Barbadian air-space as a result of the machinations of a cabal of anti-Cuban terrorists operating with the support and complicity of the USA's **Central Intelligence Agency** (CIA).

The people of Barbados were faced with the horrendous task of retrieving the mangled, dismembered bodies of the 73 victims from the Caribbean Sea, and of coming to terms with the shock and trauma that this unprecedented act of terrorism generated in our small 166 square mile nation.

But in spite of the justifiable feelings of national outrage, the primary instincts of the Barbadian people and government led them to pursue a civilized approach of legality and due process of law! This manifested itself in the immediate and successful efforts of the Barbadian authorities to secure the arrests in Trinidad of the two Venezuelan functionaries who had planted the bomb and their two CIA financed handlers in Venezuela; the sending of Barbadian Police investigators to Trinidad to interrogate these two malefactors; the setting up in Barbados of a Commission of Enquiry into the tragedy; the engaging with the governments of Cuba, Venezuela and Trinidad and Tobago on determining the most appropriate way of dealing with the captured terrorists; and the making of a collective decision to put the four captives on trial in Venezuela.

It should be noted that both Barbadian and Cuban Police and intelligence personnel travelled to the locations in which the culprits were being held in Trinidad and Venezuela, not for the purpose of assassinating them or attempting to assassinate them, but for the purpose of ensuring that a proper legal process was put in place!

This is how civilized nations, governments and people behave! They do not succumb to the 'law of the jungle' nor to the evil philosophy that 'might makes right'.

Almost 30 years after the tragic events of 6th October 1976, Mr. Ricardo Alarcon, the President of Cuba's **National Assembly of People's Power**, paid the ultimate compliment to the governments and people of Barbados and Trinidad & Tobago when he publicly stated that "Barbados and Trinidad, it must be said, acted with great dignity and honour," and acknowledged the "meticulous, rigorous, serious investigation done by people who respect themselves, people from countries that are small but which know how to respect their sovereignty."

It is because of this history and background that we, the people of little Barbados, can and must point at 'the Emperor' and tell him that he is naked!

Chapter 24

FORWARD - IN THE NAMES
OF TRAYVON & I'AKOBI

THE United States of America (USA) is currently convulsed with raging debates and public protests over the extra-judicial killing of **Trayvon Martin**, a 17-year-old African-American youth, and the reluctance of the White dominated criminal justice system to try Martin's killer.

The unarmed Martin was shot to death in the Florida town of Sanford by one George Zimmerman, a white 'neighbourhood watch' coordinator. Apparently, Zimmerman witnessed the hoodie-clad teenager walking through a middle-class neighbourhood, and immediately jumped to the conclusion that Martin was a criminal, leading to a confrontation with Martin, and ultimately to the teenager's death!

At the heart of this outrageous and tragic situation is the phenomenon known as '**Racial Profiling**', an institutionalised racist practise that, since the days of slavery, has been used to target black men and women in the USA.

But who would have thought that in the year 2012, the phenomenon of 'Racial Profiling' would still be so alive and well in Barack Obama's USA?

Well, let it be noted that Barbados has played a role in trying to encourage the USA to combat this evil practise of 'Racial Profiling'!

It was way back in the year 2001, during preparations for the **United Nations World Conference Against Racism** (UNWCAR) at UN headquarters in Geneva, that the Vice-President of the USA's second largest black civil rights organisation, the **National Urban League** (NUL), approached me and requested that I assist the NUL to draft a resolution on 'Racial Profiling' and to give it the state sponsorship it needed to get adopted by the UN.

Of course, my first reaction was to ask why the NUL was approaching the government of little Barbados, rather than its own, powerful, U.S. government. And it was explained to me that the U.S. government would never publicly admit in an international forum that the USA was afflicted by the serious racist practice of 'Racial Profiling'.

So, our 'little' Barbados did help to draft and to sponsor the following United Nations resolution:

> "The UN World Conference Against Racism urges States to design, implement and enforce effective measures to eliminate the phenomenon popularly known as 'racial profiling' and comprising the practice of police and other law enforcement officers relying, to any degree, on race, colour, descent or national or ethnic origin as the basis for subjecting persons to

> investigatory activities or for determining whether an individual is engaged in criminal activity."

This resolution is now paragraph 72 of the **Durban Programme of Action** that emerged out of the UNWCAR! And if the government of the USA had not walked out of the **World Conference Against Racism,** and had instead taken steps to seriously implement this resolution over the past decade, perhaps Trayvon Martin would still be alive today.

But we in Barbados are not ourselves immune from this type of criminal profiling. A case in point is the death of the late **I'Akobi Maloney**. In analysing the causes of Maloney's death, the Barbados Coroner noted that the tragic sequence of events was put in place by a St. Lucy resident who simply saw a dreadlocked Rastafarian walking along the St. Lucy coast and immediately jumped to the conclusion that he was involved in illicit drug activity and summoned the Police. The end result of such social/religious profiling was the death of I'Akobi.

A few of us are determined to ensure that I'Akobi Maloney must not have died in vain, and we have therefore tried to extract something positive from his death by referring the issue of 'Rasta Profiling' to the 'Inter-American Commission on Human Rights'. But alas, no massive Barbadian popular movement for societal change has mobilized around I'Akobi's death, as is the case in the USA with Trayvon's death.

To their credit, the American people have bypassed

their useless black President who, after almost four years of his presidency, has totally failed to address the issue of racism, and they are now in the process of establishing a powerful people's movement to combat racism and 'racial profiling'.

Surely this is a sign of the times, and a wake-up call for all the masses of ordinary people of our Americas region. The **Occupy Wall Street** movement and the **Justice For Trayvon** movement are showing us a way forward.

This is the time for masses of ordinary people to mobilise and to exert 'People Power' to deal with the accumulated injustices and corruption of our societies— the racism, the discriminatory profiling, the corporate greed and corruption, the social inequalities, the unjust impositions on the poor.

People, it is time to wake up and do something positive with and for your society!

Chapter 25

REASONING WITH THE YOUTH

THE call to wake up and do something positive with and for our society goes out to all Barbadians in general, but it is especially directed at the youth of our nation. And if the youth are to assume the onerous but critical duty of taking responsibility for the future progress of Barbados, then they will have to grapple with and transcend our extremely dysfunctional political and governance system.

The political and governance system of Barbados is controlled by just two organizations: the Democratic Labour Party (DLP) and the Barbados Labour Party (BLP). And when Barbadian young people look at the political and governance system they don't really see themselves—their concerns, interests or aspirations—reflected in the system.

Once every five years, when elections are called, the DLP and BLP approach young people with concerts, promises, t-shirts and hundred dollar bills on Election Day. The DLP and BLP seem to think that young people are not really interested in public affairs and that the best way to deal with them is to hype them up with music and entertainment and to bribe the poorer young people with money.

If we continue like this our future will be very bleak. In fact, many young people are already sensing that, under the present scheme of things, there is not much of a future for them in Barbados.

Well, the only way to change any of this is for the young people of Barbados to take control of a piece or portion of the political and governance system. There is no reason why, just as you have a DLP and a BLP, you could not also have a third entity that is largely made up of and controlled by young people—with some support, encouragement and guidance from older persons that the youth trust and respect.

Of course, we would not want this entity to be just a copy of the DLP and BLP. That would not make any sense, and would not be helpful to the young people of Barbados. Rather, it must be a different type of organization; one that is more relevant to the current age; one that is more reflective of a spirit of openness, honesty, helpfulness, sharing and respect; and one that is more oriented to the youth and their future.

The first step forward in this mission is to remind the youth of Barbados that, contrary to the impression given by the BLP and DLP, politics and public affairs can be very interesting, exciting, uplifting and fulfilling if they are approached in the right way and with the right spirit. Therefore, we are not talking about the traditional type of politics—the politics of one party constantly attacking the other; the politics of plenty idle talk in Parliament that means little or nothing; the politics of ministers of government dressing up in suit and tie and pompasetting while trying to keep ordinary Barbadians dependent on them and having to beg them for hand-outs; or the politics of being financed behind the scenes by rich people, and buying votes on Election Day.

Instead of the traditional type of politics, we would suggest that our young people get involved in:

- **Exploring and getting to know their cultural heritage as Barbadian and Caribbean people—** their history, music, poetry, literature, folklore, physical landscape, dramatic plays, films, dances, nation language, craft work and visual arts, and allowing that heritage to anchor, guide and inspire them;

- **Working out a new system for governing Barbados** that is fairer and that allows the people to be more involved, to contribute their talents, and to have a greater say in how things are done;

- **Brainstorming ideas for a new national economic development programme** that is built firmly upon the talents and energies of the youth of Barbados as the single greatest resource that our country possesses;

- **Working out a new concept of development for Barbados—**a concept in which development is about us looking at our own country and society; identifying what resources exist in our country and society; and taking hold of these national resources ourselves and doing something positive with them and with ourselves;

- Developing a more appropriate, environmentally friendly and self-sustaining style of living for ourselves in Barbados;
- Brainstorming ideas for transforming our education system into one in which all Barbadian children and teenagers are treated as sacred beings who must be nurtured and given every form of assistance to develop their potential and to be prepared not merely for a job, but for life itself;
- Collaborating with other young people across the Caribbean to work out plans and initiatives for the establishment of a multi-territory Caribbean nation and economy that will offer new life opportunities and a greater sense of cultural strength and national dignity;
- Collaborating with other young people from across the fast developing region of Latin America to work out ideas for a new relationship with Latin America that will bring benefits and career opportunities for the youth of Barbados;
- Brainstorming ideas for the fostering of a more fair, just and equal society in Barbados, and for a social structure that properly attends to the health and housing needs of the Barbadian people; and
- Collaborating with black youth all over the world in pursuing a campaign for 'reparations' or compensation for the losses suffered during the centuries of slavery and colonialism, and for rebuilding the black man's civilization.

If young Barbadians find this type of political

programme to be relevant, appealing and worthwhile, then we would suggest that they come together with their friends and colleagues to establish committees—People's Committees—to work on this ten point political programme.

Such youth-based 'People's Committees' can be established all over Barbados, and can derive their names from the geographical district in which they are based, or from the institution or organisation on which they are based. For example, you could have the 'Bank Hall People's Committee' or the 'Barbados Community College People's Committee'.

A convenient minimum number of persons for the establishment of a People's Committee would be ten persons, since each person could undertake the lead responsibility for one item of the ten point programme.

A 'People's Committee' would exercise its own initiative and would pursue the 10 point programme as it sees fit, but of course, the various People's Committees would also relate to each other and hold discussions and meetings together, and in this way, they would constitute a broad-based mass youth political movement. Furthermore, having such a structure of collaboration in place would facilitate the staging of various events and projects related to the ten point programme, as well as the launching of youth-run programmes to assist the poor and vulnerable sectors of our society.

If the young people of Barbados were to make such an effort, they would, at the very least, accomplish the positive mission of moving the youth, as a constituency, some distance away from the manipulative and corrupting embrace of a cynical two-party political system. In addition, and they would have put themselves in a position to make a critical intervention in the political process that just might be potent enough to so influence the national vision and agenda that it enables our country to redirect its trajectory to a more creative, honest and life-affirming path.

Chapter 26

A BATTLE FOR THE SOUL OF BARBADOS

WHEN Barbados' Prime Minister Freundel Stuart and his Democratic Labour Party (DLP) colleagues made that fateful decision to dismantle Barbados' 50 year old 'Democratic Socialist' tradition of providing free university education to the young people of Barbados, they re-introduced to the national agenda the truly momentous issue of what type of society should Barbados be?

From the very beginnings of Barbados' history as a slave society in 1627, there was a strata of the Barbadian population that was determined to ensure that Barbados would always be a non-egalitarian class society. As far as they were concerned, there were no fundamental human rights to education, health care, housing, nutrition or other elements of human well-being. On the contrary, they believed that the existence of unequal classes and social groups is the natural order of society, and that for a society to function effectively the members of that society must practise the values of individual self-interest and competitiveness among themselves.

The social forces that subscribe to that type of ideology comprise the traditional white planter and merchant classes of Barbados; their modern day equivalents in the form of Barbados' 21st century elite business class; and a number of black middle-class and professional collaborators.

Historically, that vision of Barbadian society produced a Barbados of severe inequalities, lack of opportunity, economic stagnation, and punishing poverty for the masses of black Barbadians! It was (and is) a vision of Barbados that could never countenance the idea of poor black children being given free university education.

But that vision of a class-ridden, 'survival-of-the-fittest' type of Barbados was always challenged. It was challenged in the days of slavery by such heroes as Bussa, Washington Franklyn, Nanny Gregg, Sarah Ann Gill and Samuel Jackman Prescod, and in the modern period by the '**Labour Movement**' that emerged in 1937, and that went on to struggle for a more egalitarian society under the leadership of men like Wynter Crawford, Grantley Adams, Frank Walcott and Errol Barrow.

And, of course, the alternative vision of Barbadian society that these progressive social forces held aloft was that of a society that reflected the values of equality, community, social inclusion, human well-being, fairness, cooperation, and an equality of opportunity that engendered the maximum development of the human potential of the society.

Needless to say, the full vision of the 1930s generation of labour leaders—the Clement Paynes and Israel Lovells—was compromised in many important respects by the Adamses and Barrows, and has never been fully realized. But there were at least three spheres in which admirable justice was done to that 1937 vision, and these were: the creation of a 'Mixed Economy' characterised by both private businesses and government or people-owned enterprises; the establishment of an accessible and inexpensive public health care system; and most importantly, the provision of 'free' education from the Primary to the Tertiary level.

In 1985, less than two years before his untimely death, the Right Excellent Errol Barrow explained the significance and critical importance of free education as follows:

> "I have always thought of myself as a Socialist in the general terms of the British Labour Party... Democratic Socialism is about planning and equality of opportunity. It has always been fundamental to our basic philosophy. We have tried to ensure, so far as possible, that every child born in Barbados has the opportunity to develop the talents with which the Lord has blessed it regardless of the family circumstances into which it happened to be born.
>
> That is why one of the first things we did when we won the Government was to decree that secondary education (and subsequently tertiary education) would be free of charge... The success of that programme has been proven for all to see—some of the beneficiaries are now amongst our most vociferous critics."

And, as Mr. Barrow intimated, there were always reactionary social forces in Barbados that were hostile to our achievement of a Mixed Economy, 'free' health care and education, and to the vision of the type of Barbadian society that these achievements were leading to.

These social forces have been planning, plotting and conniving for many years now to dismantle these achievements, and it seems that they have now found willing allies in the current governmental administration.

Indeed, as far back as March 1990 the 'Barbados Chamber of Commerce and Industry' (BCCI) joined together with the multi-national accounting firm of 'Ernst & Young' to stage a private sector convocation on reforming the Barbadian economy and society, and this is what they had to say in their document entitled *Post Conference Summary*:

"Government expenditure is excessive, unsustainable and is at a level which is causing negative returns... Some suggested areas for reduction:

- Reduce scope of welfare services including health
- Eliminate free tertiary education
- Introduce entitlement programmes (means testing)

A planned programme of privatisation is desirable... Targets for privatisation should include both profitable and unprofitable enterprises and be extended to central government services... Suggested targets include: CBC, Dairy, Transport Board, Insurance Corporation, BNB, Arawak Cement, BMC, IDC factories, revenue collection, Barbados Mills, Port Authority etc."

Well, if we examine the record of the 23 years that have passed since March 1990, we will see just how successful these elitist forces have been in implementing their agenda for Barbados and in achieving their vision of an elite dominated society. To start with, they have been successful in securing privatisation of approximately 50% of the targets on their privatisation list: the Pine Hill Dairy, Insurance Corporation of Barbados, Arawak Cement Plant, Barbados National Bank and Barbados Mills.

And, even more alarmingly, since the advent of the current governmental administration, they have started to dismantle both the system of 'free' health care and the system of 'free' tertiary education.

Sadly, it seems as if several individuals who personally benefited from Barbados' marvellous system of 'free university education' and who, as a result, have gone on to assume positions of great influence and power in our society, are now in the process of helping the wealthy elite forces of Barbados to kick down the ladder on which poor black Barbadians have been ascending over the past 50 years!

Make no mistake about it, we are now well and truly engaged in a national Civil War over what type of society Barbados is to be. Is it to be a society of equality and social inclusion—one in which the entire national population and the entire pool of taxpayers collectively bear the costs of providing critical education for our children and young people? Or is it to be a society of separation and inequality—one in which the cost of tertiary education is placed on the shoulders of the individual student and his or her immediate family, in spite of the fact that students and their families vary tremendously in terms of ownership of wealth?

I am ready to enlist in this War, and I know who the enemies are and the type of Barbados that they want to foist upon us all. I will resist them with all the strength and energy that I possess!

Chapter 27

A NEW MODEL OF GOVERNANCE FOR BARBADOS

DURING the 2013 General Election season the Democratic Labour Party (DLP) spent millions of dollars on a propaganda campaign that was designed to convince the people of Barbados that the DLP was profoundly committed to maintaining all existing jobs in the public sector of Barbados.

They used the millions of dollars given to them by un-named wealthy 'donors' on advertisements and public meetings in which they assured that a vote for the DLP was a vote to preserve public sector jobs, and that a vote for the opposition Barbados Labour Party (BLP) would be a vote for privatisation of public entities and loss of public sector jobs!

They even went beyond this and actually created additional public sector jobs during the year leading up to the General Elections.

Now, a few months later, the leaders of the DLP have callously and unabashedly informed Barbadians that there are too many persons employed in the public sector, that over 5,000 of these jobs are being cut, and that—in the words of Minister Donville Inniss—the decision to cut these jobs was not a tough decision to make!

Well, there you have it! Once again you have been taken for a ride. Yet again, you have been provided with incontrovertible proof that your political system is a sham. It is a sham because it is dominated by 'big money' anonymously given; it is characterised by expensive propaganda campaigns rather than reasoned argument; it is becoming progressively dependent on the corrupt practice of exchanging hard cash for votes; and it is shot through with a pronounced lack of accountability to the people.

So, what is the solution? Is it to punish the DLP with your vote at the next General Election? That is an understandable reaction, and is certainly a legitimate part of the solution, but it cannot be the totality of the solution. In addition to punishing the DLP, we have to reform the very system of governance itself.

We have to set our hearts and minds on reforming our political system, and molding it into a new system that is much more 'people participatory' and much more accountable to us, the people of Barbados.

And clearly, the first step in the process is to devise a new 'model' for our political system—a 'model' around which we can all mobilize.

I would therefore like to propose to my fellow Barbadians that a useful place to start in looking for a new model for our political system, is the nation of Switzerland—one of the smallest countries in Europe, but one of the most democratic and successful nations in the entire world.

As some of us may be aware, the nation of Switzerland

is actually a confederation of some twenty-three sovereign constituent states. Most of these states, though quite small by international standards, are larger and more populous than Barbados. But what is most noteworthy about these small states that comprise the **Confederation of Switzerland** is that they are regarded as exemplars of people-participatory democracy.

So, let us examine the Swiss model of people-participatory democracy, and consider to what extent we can adopt it here in Barbados. The features of the model that I would propose for consideration are as follows:

A Multi-Party System

Unlike Barbados, with its two large monopoly political parties, the citizens of the small Swiss states operate at least eight political parties, each of which represents a distinct strand of socio-economic-political thought. These parties bear such names as Social Democrats, Liberal Party, Radical Democratic Party, Christian Democratic Party, Swiss People's Party, Alliance of Independents, Labour Party and the Party of Progressive Organisations. The existence of this range of political parties affords Swiss citizens maximum opportunities for participation in the political system, and ensures that all significant strains of opinion that exist in the national population find expression in the national Parliament.

Proportional Representation

The main reason such a range of political parties continues to exist in the small Swiss states is that these states practise an electoral system based on 'Proportional Representation'. Under a 'Proportional Representation' system, small political parties that are unable to win constituency seats in 'first-past-the-post' electoral contests, are still allocated seats in the national Parliament on the basis of the total number of votes they amass across the entire country. Barbados could easily establish a 'Proportional Representation' system by conflating our House of Assembly and Senate into one Chamber, and by permitting the 21 Senatorial seats to be allocated to representatives of the various political parties on a proportional basis.

Direct Election of Ministers of Government

The various ministers of government in the small Swiss states are directly elected by the people themselves. Thus, a General Election consists not only of an election of citizens to sit in the House of Assembly, but also an election of citizens to the various offices that exist in the separate institution known as 'the Executive', or in our parlance: 'the Cabinet'. Under such a system, the various political parties (or groups of citizens) put up candidates for the posts of Minister of Agriculture, Minister of Finance, Minister of Education etc., and the citizens vote for who they would wish to see heading such ministries.

No Cock-Fight Politics

Rather than a General Election in a Swiss state producing a governing party and an opposition party that are perpetually at each other's throats, it is actually designed to produce a national 'Chamber of legislators' drawn from all of the significant political parties, and a separate 'Cabinet of Ministers' that also comprises representatives of several political parties. The 'Chamber of Legislators' is mandated to proceed with the task of making laws and regulations for the state, while the 'Cabinet of Ministers' is expected to get on with the task of running the various government ministries. Furthermore, the two institutions 'check and balance' each other, with the plans and proposals of the Executive having to be approved by the Legislative Chamber, and the Ministers playing a key role in initiating and vetting legislation and regulations.

A Collegial Head of Government

Under the Swiss system, the Cabinet Ministers select or elect one of their members to assume the role of chairperson of the Cabinet and therefore 'Prime Minister' or 'Head of Government' of the state. However, the selected chairperson's term is usually a limited one, and other ministers are also given the opportunity to serve as Prime Minister during the term of a government. In a very real sense therefore, there is a collegial Head of Government, with the entire cabinet performing this role.

People Power

Under the Swiss model the people are not relegated to only expressing power once every five years! Rather, they are given a controlling power which may be expressed at any time through such instruments as the Referendum, the **Veto**, and the **Popular Initiative**. Certain legal enactments, especially decisions on the Constitution, have to be decided upon by the people via what is known as a '**Compulsory Referendum**'. In the case of other legislation, a certain percentage of the electorate, either by collecting signatures or petitioning the Parliament, are entitled to demand that such legislation be put to a national vote of the people. And in similar vein, the Popular Initiative permits a certain number of voters to submit their own proposals for legislation (legislative initiatives) or for constitutional amendments (constitutional initiatives), and to demand that they be submitted to the electorate. These instruments are also used to give the people a controlling power over government expenditure, since state expenditure beyond a certain amount must, at the request of a given number of petitioning voters, be submitted to the people for approval.

Power of Recall

In situations in which a particular legislator, a minister, or indeed an entire administration is floundering or performing badly, Swiss citizens may also use the petition to gather sufficient signatures to force the government to stage a Referendum or popular vote on whether such a legislator/minister should be recalled, or Parliament prorogued and new elections held.

This then is a model of democratic, people participatory government that already exists and that has been tried and tested over a two hundred year period. It is also a model of government that has allowed Switzerland to emerge as one of the most progressive countries in the world.

Isn't it time for Barbadians to make a move on this critical issue of reforming our model of national governance?

Chapter 28

AN EMANCIPATION DAY VISION

AS we near the end of these reflections, I would like to return to the issue with which we started—the issue of Emancipation. On the 1st of August 1998 I was granted the tremendous privilege of sharing an Emancipation Day platform with the great Fidel Castro, the then President of Cuba. I would now like to share with the youth of Barbados and the Caribbean the speech that I delivered that morning at the foot of Barbados' famous Emancipation Statue:

"As I walked up the slope of the ABC Highway this morning and I witnessed the thousands of our people converging upon the Bussa Statue, it occurred to me that what we are experiencing in these days is the birth of a new Barbadian.

Significant numbers of Barbadians are leaving the old hang-ups and inferiority complexes behind, and are moving into a new consciousness, a new sense of themselves, a new understanding of their history and destiny.

The Guyanese poet, Martin Carter, expressed this idea beautifully when he said:

"I come from the Nigger yard of yesterday
Leaping from the oppressor's hate
And the scorn of myself;

From the agony of the dark hut in the shadow
And the hurt of things,
From the long days of cruelty and the long
Nights of pain,

Down to the wide streets of tomorrow, of the
next day
Leaping I come, who cannot see will hear..."

Yes, a new Barbadian is emerging, and those who cannot of their own accord see and appreciate the beauty and rightness of this progressive development, will surely have to hear about it from us.

Those who are so mean-spirited that they still seek to minimize and subtly justify slavery; those who would deny us the right to 'grieve' for the sufferings of our forefathers, and to celebrate the triumphs of our history; those who would deny us the right to grow into the new, conscious, self-aware, liberated black men and women that we must become; these people will have to hear from us!

And we are telling them that we have long gone past the stage where we are going to hold back and stifle ourselves and restrict our growth, simply because a few wealthy and comfortable individuals are feeling some level of discomfort with the powerful spectacle they see unfolding before their eyes.

We are a mature people—32 years into our

Independence and 164 years into our Emancipation from physical slavery, and we know what is in our own best interest. And we know therefore that the time has come for us to complete our emancipation as a people. There are several critical things that we must do in order to complete our emancipation process, and I propose to itemise a few of them here this morning.

I therefore make bold to say that our emancipation will only be complete and sustainable if we correct the existing defects in our national secular and religious symbolism!

How, for example, can we justify still having the Queen of England as our Head of State? After all, it was the institution of the British Monarchy that was responsible for our enslavement and colonization.

I say, let us remove the Queen from the position of Head of State of Barbados, and let us elevate one of our own to that high secular office.

Similarly, how can our churches justify foisting upon our people images of almighty God that were created in Europe, by Europeans, for the use and benefit of Europeans. We are the only people in the world who aren't allowed to conceive of our God and saviour through the prism of our own being and culture, and we must stop inflicting this unnatural damage on ourselves!

Secondly, we need to reconnect ourselves to the continent of Africa economically, culturally and politically!

Our enslavers recognized that our links to Africa were a source of strength for us and therefore did everything in their power to break these links, in order to weaken us.

We must therefore be intelligent enough to recognize that we can only strengthen ourselves by re-establishing these links.

It is vitally important as well that we recognise that we fought for and achieved Emancipation as a regional project, and that we can only sustain and deepen it on a regional basis.

As we are all aware, none of us achieved our freedom from physical slavery alone. It was the collective resistance of our ancestral freedom fighters in Haiti, Cuba, Jamaica, Barbados, Guyana, the United States of America and many other territories that so subverted and weakened the system of slavery that emancipation became an inevitability.

The lesson therefore is that if we strive collectively, we will achieve collectively! Let us therefore embrace our brothers and sisters of Cuba and South Africa. Let us embrace the Commander-In-Chief, President Fidel Castro who is here with us today and our dear Comrade Bhenghu of South Africa who is also visiting with us.

And let us resolve to build new relationships of Caribbean, and Pan-African and Third World solidarity and unity, as we strive to complete the process of emancipation.

And finally, we must recognise that the ideological foundation of our emancipation is social equality and social justice!

Our black ancestors were all slaves together. And many

of our white ancestors were white indentured servants. In a sense, they experienced a common type of equality at the bottom of the ladder. Many of them experienced a common oppression.

We must therefore establish a social ideology that says that we will rise together; not one rising at the expense of ten others.

We, the victims of inequality and exploitation, must not ourselves create a social order that fosters inequality and the exploitation of our brothers and sisters!

Yes, as a people we are leaving the nigger yard behind.

> "From the nigger yard of yesterday we come with our burdens. To the world of tomorrow we turn with our strength."

Chapter 29

TIME TO DO OUR BEST WORK

ON the 5th of July 2008 I had the privilege of delivering the feature address at the graduation ceremony of Harrison College, a 275-year-old educational institution that is regarded as one of Barbados' leading secondary schools.

I now therefore conclude these 'Reasonings" with the youth by reproducing the text of my remarks:

"Any opportunity to speak to and interact with an audience of our young people is invaluable and must be embraced. And so, when I received the invitation to address this graduation ceremony I knew that it had to take priority over my other commitments.

This therefore meant that I had to cut short my participation in the important Assembly of Caribbean People conference which is currently being held in Havana, Cuba and rush home to Barbados.

I was at the conference in Cuba with a Barbados youth delegation which, you would be intrigued to learn, included eight Harrison College students or former students out of a total of eleven youth delegates—a very impressive ratio indeed.

Now, I am conscious of the fact that I wear several

hats here this evening: an attorney-at-law of many years' experience, a political figure involved in the public life of Barbados, the parent of one of the graduates, and of course, an old scholar of Harrison College.

I think however that it is my old scholar hat that I will opt for, as I seek to speak to you from the vantage point of one who, some thirty years ago, trod the same path that you are on now; one who was subjected to very similar life and educational experiences that you were subjected to.

But, I hasten to emphasize 'similar' experiences, not the 'same' experiences! Clearly, the experience of going through adolescence and growing to adulthood in the Barbados of the 1970s is not the same as going through these phases in the first decade of the 21st century. And of course, the experience of being a student at Harrison College in the 1970's cannot be the same as the experience of being a Harrison College student in the 21st century.

I recall that some time last year, a panel discussion was held on Mr. Ralph Jemmott's recently published *History of Harrison College*, and that several discussants were proposing that Harrison College's golden age was in the past, in the 1940s or 50s, when the school was the perfect example of the colonialist, tropical version of the English grammar school. I, for my part, dared to contradict this and suggested that far from looking back to the race and class ridden colonialist past as a Golden Age, that the school is now developing a greater Barbadian nationalist consciousness and a more appropriate social and cultural identity, and that its best years are yet to come!

I therefore want to say that your generation of students has made its mark on the school and has taken it forward. You have deepened and added value and substance to the culture, nationalist spirit, institutional life and traditions of the school. And you must be given credit for having lived up to your responsibilities and improved the legacy left to you by previous generations of students.

Earlier I remarked that eight out of eleven members of the Barbados youth delegation in Cuba hailed from Harrison College. In my day that would have been inconceivable! When my colleagues and I graduated in 1979 we arranged a visit to the Caribbean island of Trinidad, it would never have entered our minds to visit revolutionary Cuba!

I recall that when I first spoke to the Harrison College students about going to Cuba and visiting the Che Guevera monument, I saw a gleam of recognition light up their countenances. Clearly, they had been taught things in school that my generation had never been taught!

So I am confident that the school is moving in the right direction and that good and progressive things are happening. Thus, it would be folly for us to look back to the colonial era as a Golden Age; rather, we must move forward to fulfill our own nationalist destiny.

You graduates therefore deserve a hearty round of applause from all of us gathered here! Much was given to you by the Barbadian society; you were given the opportunity to attend the institution that this society considers to be its most prestigious educational institution; and not only did you make good use of that opportunity, but you also preserved and helped to further the evolution and development of the institution.

All of you graduates gathered here this evening came through and absorbed your seven years of educational instruction and discovery at Harrison College, and you are now graduating as members of the newest group of young intellectuals of our Barbadian society.

Yes, I use the word 'intellectual' very deliberately! You are all intellectuals, and I want to spend a few minutes talking to you about the joy, responsibility and duties of being an intellectual in a developing country.

When Benjamin Franklin, Thomas Jefferson and the other founding fathers of the Republic of the United States of America were preparing themselves to smash the British colonial system and to establish a new society, they issued a Declaration of Independence in which they dedicated their new society to guaranteeing "life, liberty and the pursuit of happiness."

What was new in this formulation was the concept of "the pursuit of happiness." John Locke and the other founders of British Liberalism had argued that the legitimate role of government was to protect "life, liberty and property." But the American founding fathers substituted the concept of "pursuit of happiness" for "property." (Perhaps somebody should give George Bush, Dick Cheney and the other capitalist 'maguffies' who go around the world stealing other people's property and causing great unhappiness, a lesson in American history!)

Anyhow, the concept of the pursuit of happiness goes back to the German philosopher, Gottfried Wilhelm Leibniz, who saw 'happiness', not in terms of acquiring property or indulging in hedonistic sensual pleasures, but in human beings fulfilling their innate and God-given potential and purpose in life.

And at the heart of this innate human-ness is the intellect—the unique capacity of men and women for thinking, for cognition, for mental creativity: our capacity to use our human intellect to penetrate to and comprehend the universal principles or laws that govern the universe and that govern life on earth in all of its dimensions.

The only creatures capable of doing that are human beings! And when we do that, and use the knowledge derived to improve or further develop God's creation, then we are fulfilling our potential and purpose as human beings, and are pursuing happiness.

I therefore want to encourage all of you to pursue and appreciate the joys of the intellect! The joy of re-enacting and re-discovering in your own mental processes the great intellectual discoveries of mankind. The joy of conquering new areas of knowledge. The joy of thinking, of playing with ideas, of making new discoveries, and of deploying ideas.

Do not become a utilitarian who is only interested in education in so far as it helps him or her to qualify for a job! Rather, be passionately interested in knowledge as the expression of your highest human potential. This world, this Caribbean, this Barbados, desperately needs men and women who are passionately interested in knowledge and truth!

I can well recall several of my own personal experiences of intellectual enlightenment here at Harrison College. Two experiences that vividly come to mind are discovering, quite by chance, in the Harrison College library, Dr. Eric Williams' *British Historians and the West Indies* and Samuel Selvon's *Ways of Sunlight* and, as a result, having opened up for me the world of erudite, anti-imperialist historiography and the wonderfully engaging and self-revealing world of Caribbean literature.

I therefore urge you to see yourselves as intellectuals, and to take upon yourselves the challenge of leading a revolution of the intellect in our society, a former slave and colonial society that has often been derided as being anti-intellectual.

And I do not mean that in an elitist way! I am not here suggesting any form of elitism! In fact, just the opposite! The gift of the intellect is the gift of all men and women. And one of the evil things that our class-ridden society has done is to erect a false and degrading division between so-called 'mental' labour and 'manual' labour.

Therefore, your job, as you pursue the joys of the intellect, as you combat the anti-intellectualism of our society, and as you seek to transform Barbados into a society of ideas and creative thinking, part of your job is to demolish the artificial and unnecessary barriers between so-called 'mental' and 'manual' labour.

I, for one, strongly believe that it is possible to make

the world of ideas, the world of culture, history, literature and philosophy, and even the world of science, accessible to all categories of labour in our society. Permit me, therefore, to fortify this point by quoting from a tribute which I penned upon receipt of news of the untimely death of Barbados' greatest natural scientist— Professor Oliver Headley.

This is what I said on that occasion:

> "…whenever I got the chance to speak about the tremendous contributions that African people on the continent and in the Diaspora have made to science over the centuries, it always gave me great pleasure to be able to cite Professor Oliver Headley as a living example of our unquestioned ability in this sphere of knowledge and activity.

> And I am convinced that of all our scientists, Professor Headley, because of his specialization in the field of solar energy, was the one best placed to make a fundamental breakthrough in infusing our people with a scientific sensibility and passion.

> I don't know if Professor Headley ever read the work of Simone Weil, the enigmatic French philosopher of the 1930s and 40s, but in a 1943 memorandum to the exiled French Government of General de Gaulle, she explained the necessity and methodology of bringing science to the French people as an integral part of post-war reconstruction:

"Science should be presented to rural people and urban workmen in very different ways. In the case of urban workmen, it is natural that mechanics should occupy the foremost place. In that of rural people, everything should be centered around the wonderful cycle whereby solar energy, poured down into plants, is retained in them by the action of chlorophyll, becomes concentrated in seeds and fruits, enters into man in the form of food or drink, passes into his muscles and spends itself on preparing the soil. Everything connected with science can be situated around this cycle, for the notion of energy is at the heart of everything. Were the thought of this cycle to sink deep into the minds of French peasants, it would permeate their labour with poetry."

I am sure Professor Headley would have seen his vocation in similar terms—bringing light and poetry to our people."

The other major point I wish to make to you is that the time has come when all of us who care about this Barbados, this Caribbean, this world, need to do our best work, now!

Make no mistake about it, our civilization has come to a critical crossroads, and is facing what is perhaps its most fundamental crisis of the past 100 years. Put simply, we are now in the beginning phase of a profound international economic and financial crisis, an energy crisis, a food crisis, an ecological and environmental crisis, and a moral and ethical crisis—a veritable system of multiple crises, creating one single systemic crisis of our civilization!

And you, the new and upcoming generation of leaders and shapers of our society, need to respond to this existential crisis by doing your best work ever!

You must not do like previous generations and be content to slavishly look for and follow leadership and trends from 'over in away'—from North America and Europe.

In fact, they are the ones who are mostly responsible for the crisis, and they have very little to teach us! Instead, be prepared to look within to the best of our own history, inventions and achievements, and seek to build up and add to these foundations.

Let me delve into the realm of politics—political theory and practice—in order to give you an example of what I am talking about. The English-speaking Caribbean has produced arguably the most fertile, creative and humane political theorist of the 20th century in the form of C.L.R. James—a prolific thinker and writer who has left a body of work that can give us tremendous native insights into the political nature of our society, and the type of political arrangements that can bring out the best in us.

But even the great James does not stand alone. Marcus Garvey, George Padmore, Lloyd Best, Tim Hector, Walter Rodney, Michael Manley and Cheddi Jagan, among others, have also provided us with tremendous intellectual foundations in the sphere of politics. It is now up to your generation to build upon these foundations.

And the same can be said for the sphere of literature—

Martin Carter, Kamau Brathwaite, Lamming, Naipaul, Derek Walcott, Selvon; and for Sport, Science, Architecture, Economics, Dance, Music, and the list goes on. And mind you, I have confined myself to the English speaking Caribbean and have not even mentioned the shining lights of the Francophone, Dutch and Hispanic Caribbean.

Your challenge therefore, is to develop the self-confidence and the self-respect to investigate these foundations and to build upon them!

Another aspect of 'doing your best work' is that you must consciously set out to become the key professionals and workers who will take personal responsibility for solving the major problems facing our society.

For example, the nation of Barbados has a water distribution system that is now over 100 years old, and that is shortly going to need to be substantially replaced. And I wish to suggest that somewhere among you should be the science graduate whose ambition is to become the key hydraulic engineer who is going to solve this problem for his people.

I would like to think that one of you would see it as your personal responsibility to set out to go down in history as the loyal son or daughter who led the nation in solving this monumental problem.

Somewhere among you should be the graduate whose ambition is to be the pioneer in developing alternative energy to the next level, so as to help Barbados escape its stifling dependence on ever more expensive petroleum imports.

Somewhere among you should be the dancer who is going to consciously set out to do for Barbados what Rex Nettleford did for the Jamaica National Dance Theatre, and what Alicia Alonzo did for the National Ballet in Cuba.

Somewhere among you should be the cricketer whose ambition is to restore the once proud tradition of Barbados and West Indies cricket.

You must see it as your personal responsibility to prepare yourselves to undertake the critical tasks that are necessary if our people are going to be able to solve the fundamental problems facing them!

It is time for you to prepare yourself to do your best work for your people—for all the tens of thousands of humble tax payers and citizens who ultimately financed and provided you with your education at Harrison College, and at all the other fine secondary schools of Barbados. You have a duty to give back! You should want to give back!

Indeed, you should derive pleasure and a sense of fulfillment from giving back to your people, your community, your nation.

And in asking you to prepare to do your best work, and to rise up to exalted heights of achievement, I am not asking you to do anything that is beyond your capacities!

When I look at the record of young achievers in Barbados—George Lamming, writing his ground-breaking *In the Castle of My Skin* at 23 years of age, and demonstrating an absolute mastery of the English language; Garfield Sobers, establishing a world record of 365 not out at the age of 21 years and exhibiting the most profound understanding of the nuances of cricket; and 17-year-old Rihanna taking the international entertainment world by storm, I know that you possess the innate capacity!

Indeed, when I look at the Harrison College of today, and the education and socialization that you were given there, I know that you have been given a foundation that has rooted you and that provides you with a healthy sense of identity and a capacity to excel.

I therefore say to you and to all of the other successful young secondary school graduates of Barbados: believe in yourselves! Be true to yourselves! You are our beautiful, decent and talented young people—the flowers of our society, the pride of our nation!

Go forward and fulfill your potential!

Go forward and do justice to yourselves!"

DAVID COMISSIONG was born on the 17th April 1960 in the Caribbean island of St. Vincent. The son of a travelling Methodist Minister of Religion, David received his primary education at Tranquility Primary School in Trinidad, before attending Harrison College and the University of the West Indies (UWI) in Barbados.

He won a Barbados Exhibition in 1979 and the 'Sir Fred Phillips' academic prize at the Faculty of Law, University of the West Indies in 1981 and has been a practicing Attorney-at-law since 1984.

David Comissiong is a former Senator in the government of Barbados, and is currently the President of the opposition Peoples Empowerment Party (PEP).

He is also a founder-member and current President of the Clement Payne Movement of Barbados-one of the most important activist organizations of the Eastern Caribbean.

David has been a driving force in the Pan-African Movement over the past 20 years. He is a founder-member of the Pan-African Movement of Barbados (PAMOB), the Caribbean Pan-African Network (CPAN) and the

Global Afrikan Congress (GAC) and was an architect and the first Director of the Barbados Government's Commission For Pan-African Affairs (CPAA).

He represented the Caribbean region at the 7th Pan-African Congress in Uganda (1994), and played a key role in the United Nations' World Conference Against Racism in South Africa (2001).

Index

A

Abolition Committee, the
    45
abolitionism 47
Abolition of Slavery Act,
    the 1
Abolition Society, the 45
Adams, Sir Grantley 8,
    118
Africa 11, 16, 22, 26, 58,
    59, 62, 64, 66, 85,
    107, 155
African Colonisation
    Society, the 76
African culture 6, 10
African Diaspora, the 60,
    62, 74
African Liberation Day 73
African Methodist
    Episcopal Church,
    the 62
African National Con-
    gress, the 73
African Nationalism 93
African Nationalist Pio-
    neer Movement, the
    94
Akan society, the 38

Alarcon, Ricardo 129
Ali, Muhammad 93
Allende, Salvador 127
Allsop, Dr. Richard 36, 38
Alonzo, Dr. Alicia 168
Anglican Church, the 46
Arthur, Owen 95, 119
Assembly of Caribbean
    People, the 158
Atkins, Governor 33, 37
Australopithecus africanus
    63

B

Barbadian culture 9
Barbadian history 7, 14,
    28, 31
Barbadians 5, 13, 18, 25,
    28, 30, 34, 38, 102,
    112, 134, 153
Barbadian society 6, 91,
    98, 141, 160
Barbados 5, 13, 19, 26, 28,
    29, 31, 36, 59, 89, 96,
    98, 102, 116, 121,
    131, 134
Barbados Chamber of
    Commerce and

Industry, the 143
Barbados Cricket League,
    the 98
Barbados' Declaration of
    Independence 26
Barbados Garrison, the 16
Barbados Labour Party,
    the 90, 134, 146
Barbados Workers' Union,
    the 90
Barclay, Arthur 77
Barclay, Edwin 77
Barclay, Sarah Ann 76
Barrow, Errol 89, 112,
    113, 119, 122, 142
Barrow, Reginald 112
Beckford, George 115
Beckles, John 90
Beckles, Sir Hilary 6, 14,
    115
Bennett, Dorcas 90
Best, Lloyd 115, 166
bin Laden, Osama 126
Black Nationalism 86, 93,
    94, 114
Black Panthers, the 94
Black Power Movement,
    the 114
Black Segregation Codes
    86
Black Star Line, the 88
Black Studies 94
Blyden, Edward Wilmot
    70

Bolt, Usain 114
Brathwaite, Chrissie 90
Brathwaite, Edward
    Kamau 14, 101,
    102, 106, 108, 166
Bridgetown 13, 18, 22, 116
British Abolition of
    Slavery Act, the 1
Browne, David 14
Bush, George 161
Bussa, General 8
Bussa Rebellion 5, 7, 16,
    22, 52

C

Cadogan, Martin 92, 93,
    94
Caribbean family 115
Caribbean integration 116
Caribbean literature 163
Caribbean people 62, 99,
    112, 118, 136, 158
CARICOM 112, 119
CARIFTA 119
Carter, Henderson 14
Carter, Martin 1, 63, 153,
    166
Castro, Fidel 153, 156
Central Intelligence
    Agency (CIA) 128
Cesaire, Aime 114
Charter of Barbados, the
    26, 27
Christophe, Henri 44

Civil Rights Movement, the 94

Clarke, Bobby 14

Clarkson, Thomas 46

Clement Payne Movement, the 14, 82, 91, 94

colonialism 9, 59, 137

Coltman, Elizabeth 46

Combermere, Lord 52

Commission for Pan-African Affairs, the 172

Committee For The Abolition of The Slave Trade 42

Compulsory Referendum 151

Comrade Bhenghu 156

Confederation of Switzerland, the 148

Confederation Riots, the 7

Congress Party, the 90

Craton, Michael 51

Crawford, Wynter 90, 119

Cromwell, Oliver 28

Cuban Revolution, the 114

Cudjoe the maroon 114

Cuffy 37, 38, 40

Cummins, Hugh Gordon 90

D

Declaration of Independence, the 26, 29, 161

Democratic Labour Party, the 95, 134, 140, 146

Democratic League, the 90

Dessalines, Jean Jacques 44

DuBois, W.E.B. 71

Durban Programme of Action, the 132

Dyde, Brian 21

E

Elsa Goveia 115

emancipation 1, 5, 67, 95, 153, 156

Emancipation Act, the 1, 53

Emancipation Day 95, 153

Emancipation Proclamation, the 86

Emancipation Statue, the 101, 153

Emptage, Allan 124

English Civil War, the 28

Equiano, Olaudah 116

Ernst & Young 143

F

Fanon, Frantz 114

Fante ethnic group 38

Ford, Arnold Josiah 80
Ford, Mignon Inniss 80
Fortuna, Anna 32
Franklin, Benjamin 161
Franklyn, Washington 141

G

Garveyism 72, 87, 88, 89,
        90, 94
Garvey, Marcus 72, 78, 85,
        89, 90, 91, 92, 114,
        166
General Bussa 17
Gill, Sarah Ann 141
Girvan, Norman 115
Governor Atkins 33
Gregg, Nanny 141
Grenville, Lord 45

H

Hall, Grand Master Prince
        70, 75
Hall, Judge Gyles 32
Harrison College 158,
        163, 169
Hart, Richard 55
Headley, Professor Oliver
        164
Hector, Tim 166
Henry, Paget 9
Hochschild, Adam 45
Homo erectus 63
Homo habilis 63
Homo sapiens 64

Hooper, Anne 90

I

Industrial Revolution, the
        15, 48, 114
Inniss, Donville 146
In the Castle of My Skin
        96, 104, 168
Israel Lovell Foundation
        14, 82

J

James, C.L.R. 72, 98, 100,
        114
Jefferson, Thomas 27, 161
Jemmott, Ralph 159
Justice For Trayvon
        Movement, the 133

K

Kemet 66, 68
Kingdom of Ethiopia, the
        86
King Menes 66
King of Barbados 32, 35
Kwan Yew, Lee 122

L

Lamming, George 9, 96,
        104, 115, 168
League of Coloured People
        79
Leibniz, Gottfried
        Wilhelm 162

Lewis, Gordon 7, 115
Lewis, Sir Arthur 115
Liberia 36
Ligon, Richard 29, 31
Lincoln, Abraham 86
L'Ouverture, Toussaint 44, 114
Lovell, Israel 90
Lumumba, Patrice 127

M

Ma'at 67
Malcolm X 62, 94
Maloney, I'Akobi 132
Mandela, Nelson 95
Manley, Michael 166
Marcus Garvey Steel Shed 91
Marshall, Trevor 14
Marshall, Woodville 14
Martin, Trayvon 130, 132
McNeil, William 65
Middle Passage 106
Moody, Thomas 6
Moore, Richard B. 118
Mottley, Elombe 14

N

National Assembly of People's Power, the 129
National Democratic Party, the 95
National Urban League,

the 131
Neanderthals 64
Nettleford, Rex 168
New International Economic Order, the 60
Nile Valley civilization 66, 68
N'Krumah, Kwame 72, 73

O

Obama, Barack 130
Occupy Wall Street Movement, the 133
O'Connell, Daniel 53
O'Neale, Charles Duncan 112
Organization of African Unity, the 73

P

Padmore, George 72, 79
Pan-African Congress, the 71, 72, 172
Pan-Africanism 62, 69, 70, 75, 114
Pan-African Movement, the 74, 171
Pan-African Movement of Barbados, the 82
Pares, Richard 15
Payne, Clement 8, 14, 90, 91
Peoples Progressive

Movement 82
Pinelands Creative
Workshop, the 14
Prescod, Samuel Jackman
8, 117, 120, 141

Q

Qaddafi, Muamar 74

R

Racial profiling 130, 131,
133
racism 85, 133
Rastafarian 132
Reparations 56, 61, 62,
137
Reparations Movement,
the 61
Rihanna 96, 98
Rodney, Walter 60, 115,
166

S

Sandiford, Erskine 95
Selvon, Samuel 163
Sharpe, Granville 42
Singapore 122
Slavery 59, 61, 62, 68, 118,
130, 137, 154, 156
slave society 6, 39
Sobers, Sir Garfield 96,
114
Southern Africa Liberation
Committee, the 82

Springer, Sir Hugh 79, 90
Stanley, Earl 53
St. Ann's Garrison 16, 19
Stephen, George 46
Stuart, Freundel 140

T

Thomas Clarkson 42, 46
Thomas, Clive 115
Trans-Atlantic slave trade,
the 68
Tudor, James A. 90

U

UNDP 59
UNESCO 13, 18, 38
United Nations World
Conference Against
Racism, the 57, 131,
132, 172
United States of America,
the 12, 86, 126, 130,
156, 161
Universal Ethiopian An-
them, the 83, 90
Universal Negro Improve-
ment Association,
the 72, 87, 93
U.S. government, the 131

V

Vaughan, Sir John 20

W

Walcott, Derek 167
Washington, George 27,
    91
West India Regiment, 1st
    22
West India Regiment, 8th
    24
Wilberforce, William 42
Williams, Dr. Eric 50, 163

Williams, Henry Sylvester
    71
Workingmen's
    Association, the 90
World Heritage site 13, 18

Z

Zimmerman, George 130